THE NOBLE BEREAN
VOLUME 2

...AND THEY SEARCHED THE SCRIPTURES DAILY,
WHETHER THOSE THINGS WERE SO...

by

Thomas M. Kissinger

Straightway Publishing Company

Baton Rouge, Louisiana

The Noble Berean Series Volume 2

The Noble Berean:
And They Searched The Scriptures Daily,
Whether Those Things Were So

Copyright © 2008 by Thomas M. Kissinger
Straightway Publishing Company

For further information, contact the author through Straightway Publishing Company

Published by:
Straightway Publishing Company
Post Office Box 45212 #261
Baton Rouge, LA. 70895
Email: tkissinger01@cox.net
(225) 766-0896

Book and cover design: Rich Baldwin

The Noble Berean:
And They Searched The Scriptures Daily,
Whether Those Things Were So

By Thomas M. Kissinger

1. Author 2. Title 3. Inspiration 4. Religion
Library of Congress Control Number: 2007904055
ISBN: 978-0-9785134-2-9 (Paperback)

Printed in the United States of America

To my wife Sarah, and our children Moriah, Makayla, and Micah. I love each of you so very much. I continually pray that the God of our Lord Jesus Christ, the Father of glory, may give unto you the spirit of wisdom and revelation in the knowledge of Him!

To Louis Thompson. I truly believe you are one of the greatest men of God I will ever meet. I am fascinated by your desire to know the Lord!

To Billy Thompson. You are a great friend and teacher. The hours and hours we spend talking about God's purpose and plan are some of the most cherished moments in my life!

To Dr. Harold Lovelace. There are not many Fathers in The Faith, but you are definitely one of them. Thank you for being a mentor and Father in The Faith to me. You are a true Berean!

To Dr. Stephen Jones. Your writings are some of the most unique, clear, and concise of those in this great message of reconciliation. They have been a tremendous inspiration to me!

To Pastor David Davis. You and your wife have taught and demonstrated to me the most important principle of the Holy Scriptures, which is: God IS Love! I know that you both are true disciples of the Lord Jesus, for you teach and demonstrate the love of God to others!

To Mary Cage. One of your greatest attributes is how you earnestly contend for The Faith which was once delivered to the saints. I wish there were more like you. Thank you for your many hours of editing!

GRAND STATEMENT

*…they received the word with all readiness of mind,
and searched the Scriptures daily,
whether those things were so.*

Acts 17:11

To all those who are Bereans at heart. I appreciate you
for your willingness to receive God's Word with all readiness
of mind. Continue to search the Scriptures daily!

To all those who are yet to be Bereans.
You are invited to take a journey to the heart
of the one and true living God!

CONTENTS

PART 1 - THE AUTHENTICITY OF THE HOLY SCRIPTURES

PART 2 - GOD THE CREATOR

PART 3 - OF HIM, THROUGH HIM, AND TO HIM

PART 4 - SPEAKING THE TRUTH IN LOVE

PART 5 - THE KEY OF THE BOTTOMLESS PIT

PART 6 - ETERNITY AND TIME

PART 7 - THE PURPOSE OF PRAYER IN LIGHT
OF GOD'S SOVEREIGNTY

PART 8 - HONEST ABOUT EARNEST

PART 9 - WHY IS IT THOUGHT INCREDIBLE THAT
GOD RAISES THE DEAD?

PART 10 - THE PRECIOUS BLOOD OF CHRIST

PART 11 - EARS TO HEAR

PART 12 - CHRIST IS ALL, AND IN ALL

PART 13 - MY THOUGHTS ARE NOT YOUR THOUGHTS

PART 14 - QUALIFIED FOR THE PRIZE

PART 15 - THE GREATNESS OF GOD

INTRODUCTION

"Some writers fill pages with words that are so 'generic' that they can be taken so many different ways and thus do not arouse the reader to think in a higher level than before. Your encounter with Thomas Kissinger's writings will affect you in a way to make you become an activist when sharing what his writings have impressed upon your thoughts about the subject. They will challenge you to change from the status quo to seeing the necessity of sharing clearly the ideas proposed that you will begin searching again to see if they are "so-true" just like the Bereans.

You will see in years to come that Thomas' writings will always be in demand. The apostle Paul spoke, saying that "The Christ was The Son of God." This was a new concept for these Jews in so much that they searched the Old Testament to investigate that this was in fact the truth. They were considered of a nobler disposition, generous minded, of finer spirits, and "received The Word with all readiness of mind." Paul opened what had been a secret-mystery. It was a new idea or a revelation and they wanted to check it out. Yet some others were not as noble and did not search, so they did not know the greater things about God and His Plan. Jesus stated this same principle in Matthew 22:29, "you do err, not knowing the scriptures…"

As a writer and speaker, Thomas "talks our language, shares our experiences, and expresses our day-to-day concerns" as he leads all to become better searchers. The Bereans searched concerning "The Christ, The Son." Paul was correct for he understood the Old Testament Prophets and received revelation of The Son within himself. Thomas lays out his message clearly."

Dr. Harold Lovelace

PART 1 - THE AUTHENTICITY OF THE HOLY SCRIPTURES

The journey of the Berean (one who searches for truth) is one of continually asking, seeking, and knocking. It involves a lifelong search for truth. Many in this life are skeptical as to whether there is any such thing as truth or an ultimate reality such as God, the Bible, or His Son Jesus Christ. For the first twenty years of my life I did not believe in God or His Holy Scriptures. Then, at the age of twenty on the night of May 7, 1994, I had an encounter with the Lord Jesus Christ. I was approached by two men on the campus of Louisiana State University and had the Gospel declared to me. I had heard people all my life (here and there) speak of Jesus and that He died on the cross to save us, but this night was different. God had been preparing me for this very night. I had reached the place in my life where I began to question if there was a God. Prior to this night (while lying in bed one night) I called out to God in prayer, not knowing if He was real, or if my pathetic prayer was all in vain. I addressed Him and said that I did not know if I believed in Him or not, but that if He was real I wanted Him to prove it to me and show me the way. On the night that I was approached by the two men who told me about God's salvation and love for me, I knew that it was not a coincidence. I knew that it was a sign from God. It was all too real as they prayed with me on the corner of Chimes Street and led me into the sweet and loving arms of Jesus my Savior!

A HUNGER TO READ

Up to this point in my life I had absolutely no desire to read, but after coming to the saving knowledge of the Lord I was instantly hungry to read everything and anything I could get my hands on that pertained to God and His Kingdom. I was immediately drawn to the Holy Scriptures and devoured them day and night. I started with the book of Matthew and read straight through the entire New Testament. I then began with the book of Genesis and read through the entire Bible. After I finished I would simply go back to Genesis and start all over again. I have kept that up until this day. I cherish the Scriptures with all my heart and have come to believe that they are what they say they are and that they are indeed inspired by God. The more I read the Holy Scriptures the more I am absolutely convinced that they are authentic. In the beginning of my Christian experience I read the Scriptures and simply believed that they were true BECAUSE OF HOW THEY RADICALLY CHANGED MY LIFE AND BROUGHT DELIVERANCE TO ME. As I grew in grace and in the knowledge of the Lord I realized that I needed to take a deeper look into why I believed that they were authentic. I wanted to prove to myself and to others that BEYOND A SHADOW OF A DOUBT THE HOLY SCRIPTURES WERE REAL!

A DEEPER LOOK

As any Berean would do, I began to search daily as to whether the Bible was indeed what it claims to be, for the Bible itself states in 2nd Timothy 3:16...“All Scripture is given by inspiration of God, and is profitable for doctrine, for reproof, for correction, for instruction in righteousness: That the man of God may be perfect, thoroughly furnished unto all good works.” If the Scriptures themselves dare to make a claim such as this, then there should be ample evidence that they are what they claim to be. The apostle Peter also testifies as to the authenticity of the Holy Scriptures. 2nd Peter 1:20-21 states...“Knowing this first, that no prophecy of the Scripture is of any private interpretation. For the prophecy came not in old time by the will of man: but holy men of God spoke as they were moved by the Holy Ghost.” So...With all this in mind, let's take a look!

SOME THINGS TO CONSIDER

Since the Bible itself claims to be the very inspired words of God, we owe it to ourselves to check into these claims. Here are some things that should be considered when looking into the idea of the authenticity of the Bible: (Some of these things are just interesting to know, and some of these statements give very strong evidence that the Bible is indeed authentic.)

1. The Bible is the most widely distributed and most translated book in all of history.

2. The Bible itself claims to be the inspired Word of God.

3. The Bible, and the people who wrote the Bible, have been on the verge of extinction all through history, yet nothing could stop God's people and His Word from coming forth.

4. The discovery of the Dead Sea Scrolls validates the Holy Scriptures.

“In 1947, young Bedouin shepherds, searching for a stray goat in the Judean Desert, entered a long-untouched cave and found jars filled with ancient scrolls. That initial discovery by the Bedouins yielded seven scrolls and began a search that lasted nearly a decade and eventually produced thousands of scroll fragments from eleven caves. During those same years, archaeologists searching for a habitation close to the caves that might help identify the people who deposited the scrolls, excavated the Qumran ruin, a complex of structures located on a barren terrace between the cliffs where the caves are found and the Dead Sea. Within a fairly short time after their discovery, historical, paleographic, and linguistic evidence, as well as carbon-14 dating, established that the scrolls and the Qumran ruin dated from the third century B.C.E. to 68 C.E. They were indeed ancient! Coming from the late Second Temple Period, a time when Jesus of Nazareth lived, they are older than any other surviving Biblical manuscripts by almost one thousand years." -end quote- (This excerpt was taken from: Scrolls From the Dead Sea: The Ancient Library of Qumran and Modern Scholarship.)

The discovery of the Dead Sea Scrolls has actually given us OVERWHELMING EVIDENCE as to the authenticity of the Holy Scriptures. It is said that other caves in Qumran have produced fragments of over 170 scrolls representing parts of all books of the Hebrew Scriptures except Esther. Scholars discovered that there was remarkable agreement with the texts found (the Dead Sea Scrolls) compared to the texts found in medieval manuscripts. It is interesting to note that the Old Testament contains **many prophecies** concerning Christ and His crucifixion. With the discovery of the Dead Sea Scrolls that date back before the birth of Christ, we are clearly able to see that THESE PROPHECIES CONCERNING THE LORD JESUS CHRIST COULD NOT HAVE BEEN WRITTEN AFTER THE FACT, BUT ARE INDEED TRUE, INSPIRED, AND AMAZING PROPHECIES THAT WERE GIVEN BY GOD!

5. The Bible is historically and geographically accurate.

The New Encyclopedia Britannica states: "Archaeological criticism has tended to substantiate the reliability of the typical historical details of even the oldest periods (of Bible history) and to discount the theory that the Pentateuchal accounts (the historical records in the earliest books of the Bible) are merely the reflection of a much later period." -end quote-

In essence, it has been discovered that the people, places, and cultures of the Bible were real.

6. The Bible is honest. It candidly records the victories AND failures of God's people. It does not paint a one-sided picture as that of a fairytale or myth.

7. Science does not contradict the Bible, nor does the Bible contradict science. By the way…Here is some interesting information…

According to National Geographic News: "In a 1997 survey in the science journal *Nature,* 40 percent of U.S. scientists said they believe in God—not just a creator, but a God to whom one can pray in expectation of an answer. That is the same percentage of scientists who were believers when the survey was taken 80 years earlier." -end quote-

8. The Bible is full of prophecies that have come true. This is probably one of the most convincing arguments in favor of supporting the authenticity of the Scriptures. Have you checked into Daniel's prophecy that is referred to as "The Seventy Weeks"? IT IS AMAZING! It was a prophecy given concerning the coming of Christ hundreds of years before He was born. It pinpointed the exact year that He would be anointed as Messiah and later die for the sin of the world.

9. The overall harmony of the Bible is astounding. The Bible was written by about forty different authors over a period of about 1,600 years, yet form Genesis to Revelation, the Scriptures tell one unfolding story. That is quite remarkable!

10. The Bible has power to change lives. History is full of those who have been bettered by their belief in God and their study of the Holy Scriptures. If we took the time to mention just some of the names and testimonies of those who have been radically changed by the power of the Scriptures, then we would surely run out of space, time, and ink. LET ME STATE FOR THE RECORD…I am one of those who have been changed. Hallelujah!

SEARCHING THE SCRIPTURES DAILY

For those who are able to embrace the reality of the Holy Scriptures, it is very important that we search them daily. It is important for us as believers to know why we believe what we believe and to be able to explain ourselves in a calm and rational way. The apostle Peter told us to be ready always to give an answer to others as to the hope that is within us. I can personally say that I believe in the authenticity of the Holy Scriptures and I am confident in them that they are a revelation from God to man. Let us realize what an amazing gift that the Scriptures truly are. They should be cherished, searched, and read daily, **for this is the call of the Noble Berean.**

PART 2 - GOD THE CREATOR

"Charles Darwin's *On the Origin of Species* (published 1859) is a seminal work in scientific literature and arguably *the* pivotal work in evolutionary biology. The book's full title is *On the Origin of Species by Means of Natural Selection, or the Preservation of Favoured Races in the Struggle for Life*, while for the 6th edition of 1872 the title was changed to *The Origin of Species*. It introduced the theory that populations evolve over the course of generations through a process of natural selection. It was controversial because it contradicted religious beliefs which underlay the then current theories of biology. Darwin's book was the culmination of evidence he had accumulated on the voyage of the *Beagle* in the 1830s and expanded through continuing investigations and experiments since his return. The book contradicted then-prevailing scientific doctrines, as well as widely held religious beliefs that held the Creator ordained not only the laws of nature but also directly created kinds. The idea of supernatural design in nature served two purposes; one scientific, and the other religious. Design made nature orderly, and hence made science possible. Supernatural design also gave sanction to "the moral and religious endeavours of man." -end quote- (The following passage regarding On the Origin of Species was taken from: Wikipedia, The Free Encyclopedia.)

CREATION VS. EVOLUTION

Well...Here we go. Sooner or later we must all take a look at Darwin's "Theory" of Evolution, especially if we consider ourselves to be a Noble Berean. And so the battle rages on. The debate continues. Did we come from God the Creator, or did we evolve from apelike animals? By the way...Where did these apelike animals come from? Was there a Creator Who created all things, or did the earth just poof into existence? These are very important questions and worthy of the time and effort that it takes to arrive at the truth of the matter. If God is the Creator, then we must submit to Him in all things. If there is no God, and everything we see came from nothing, then I guess we can do whatever cranks our tractor or floats our boat. In essence, if there is no God, then we can worship ourselves and set up our own rules and laws pertaining to righteousness and morality. On the other hand, if there is a God, then we are obligated to acknowledge our Creator and to search out the purpose for our existence. Let me get right to the point...that's enough tiptoeing through the tulips. It will be our goal in this short teaching to show that GOD IS THE CREATOR, AND THAT THE TEACHING OF EVOLUTION IS AN ABSOLUTE JOKE!

The first point that must be taken into consideration is this: IT IS **IMPOSSIBLE** TO HAVE CREATION WITHOUT A CREATOR! I know that those who believe in evolution want to hear a more technical answer than this, but there is no way to answer the question of creation in a more direct manner. By making this statement we are getting to the very heart of the debate. I want you to be honest with yourself and reason with me for a minute. Is it possible to have carpentry without a carpenter? Is it possible to have plumbing without a plumber? Is it possible to have writing without a writer? I think you know the answers to these questions. As a matter of fact, the Bible gives us answers and addresses the origin of the earth and the human race. On the other hand, though, Darwin's book, The Origin of Species, gives us absolutely NO ANSWERS that actually pertain to "the origin of species."

According to *New Scientist*, "Darwin's Theory: An Exercise in Science," by Michael Ruse, June 25, 1981, p. 828:

A London *Times* writer, Christopher Booker (who accepts evolution), said this about it: "It was a beautifully simple and attractive theory. The only trouble was that, as Darwin was himself at least partially aware, it was full of colossal holes." Regarding Darwin's *Origin of Species*, he observed: "We have here the supreme irony that a book which has become famous for explaining the origin of species in fact does nothing of the kind." -end quote-

According to *The Enchanted Loom: Mind in the Universe*, by Robert Jastrow, 1981, p. 19:

Booker also stated: "A century after Darwin's death, we still have not the slightest demonstrable or even plausible idea of how evolution really took place—and in recent years this has led to an extraordinary series of battles over the whole question...a state of almost open war exists among the evolutionists themselves, with every kind of (evolutionary) sect urging some new modification." He concluded: "As to how and why it really happened, we have not the slightest idea and probably never shall." -end quote-

According to *Natural History*, "Evolutionary House-cleaning," by Niles Eldredge, February 1982, pp. 78, 81:

The scientific magazine *Discover* put the situation this way: "Evolution... is not only under attack by fundamentalist Christians, but it is also being questioned by reputable scientists. Among paleontologists, scientists who study the fossil record, there is growing dissent from the prevailing view of Darwinism." Francis Hitching, an evolutionist and author of the book *The Neck of the Giraffe*, stated: "For all its acceptance in the scientific world as the great unifying principle of biology, Darwinism, after a century and a quarter, is in a surprising amount of trouble." -end quote-

According to Francis Hitching:

"If Darwinism is truly the great unifying principle of biology, it encompasses extraordinary large areas of ignorance. It fails to explain some of the most basic questions of all: how lifeless chemicals came alive, what rules of grammar lie behind the genetic code, how genes shape the form of living things." In fact, Hitching stated that he considered the modern theory of evolution "so inadequate that it deserves to be treated as a matter of faith." -end quote-

As we have already seen, Darwin's "Theory" of Evolution is in big trouble. The reason it is in such trouble is because it is not true. It is quite ironic that the title of Darwin's book (The Origin of Species) has absolutely nothing to do with what the book is about. He never really explains the origin of species, but rather, he attempts to theorize that micro-evolution is a proof for macro-evolution, still never intelligently explaining the origin of the earth or the apelike creatures that supposedly evolved into the humans that we are today. In essence, it actually requires more faith to believe Darwin's "Theory" of Evolution than it does to simply believe the Bible.

MICRO AND MACRO-EVOLUTION

According to Eddie Snipes:

"The difference between micro and macro-evolution is a major point of confusion between the Christian worldview and the Darwinian evolution worldview in today's culture. Micro-evolution is the adaptations and changes within a species while macro-evolution is the addition of new traits or a transition to a new species. Micro-evolution is a fact that is plainly observable throughout nature. Macro-evolution is a theory that has never been observed in science. Evolutionists usually argue that those who believe in creation are ignoring the facts, however, there is nothing that evolutionists observe in science that creationists or Christians as a whole disagree with. The point of contention is not on what is observed, but the belief systems that interpret what is being observed. Nothing in the Bible contradicts science; it is the assumptions that evolutionists insert into their world view that contradict the Bible."

"Don't mistake micro-evolution for Darwinian evolution. They are not related. When a Christian says they do not believe in evolution, it is not a reference to changes in specific traits. It is a reference to changes that require crossing the DNA limitations. When the facts stare evolutionists in the face, they are reduced to either insulting those who present the evidence or they must admit their world view doesn't hold water. Evolutionists always call Christians and creationists non-thinkers because we question their illogical theories. Critical analysis is not un-intellectual, but it is unreasonable to refuse to honestly look at the whole picture painted when all the facts are presented. When someone builds their belief system around a godless world view, it leaves the realm of science and becomes a religious defense. Anyone who gets angry at the facts is not defending science, but is defending their hope that God does not exist and their hope that there is no God in which we are accountable." -end quote- (<u>Micro And Macro-Evolution Explained</u>, Eddie Snipes)

NATURAL SELECTION AND MUTATIONS

According to Doug LaPointe:

"It can be noted that natural selection as a driving mechanism for evolution is totally inadequate. Natural selection (along with mutation) is said to have caused organisms to evolve from one basic kind (animals which can reproduce with one another) into another basic kind. This is prohibited genetically since all of the information for the development of an organism has already been encoded in the DNA of its parent. Variation to organisms must remain within its basic kind. For example, genetically, a wide variety of dogs can come to exist, but a dog can never become anything other than a dog. It remains in its kind. It does not have the genetic ability to become anything more. Admitting this, evolutionists have tried to explain that natural selection happened in conjunction with mutations to the genetic code. This could not produce evolution, however, since mutations do not create new genetic potential, they just alter what is already there. Furthermore, mutations are small, random, and harmful alterations to the genetic code. This also makes evolution from mutations impossible. For example, a working wristwatch does not improve but is harmed when its inside parts are randomly altered. Natural selection also contradicts the second law of thermodynamics which states that, left to themselves, all things tend to deteriorate rather than develop, while evolution wants to go in the opposite direction. "Survival of the fittest" demonstrates only how an organism has survived, not how it has evolved." -end quote- (<u>Ten Reasons Why Creation Scientists Don't Believe In Evolution</u>, Doug LaPointe)

GOD IS THE CREATOR

The Scriptures clearly identify God as the Creator of ALL THINGS, including the heavens, the earth realm, and all that exists within them. Genesis chapter one (which states that God created the heaven and the earth) takes us through the six days of creation, stating that "God ended His work which He had made; and He rested on the seventh day from all His work which He had made (Genesis 2:2)." The Hebrew word "yohm", translated "day", can mean different lengths of time. William Wilson's *Old Testament Word Studies* includes the following: "A day; it is frequently put for time in general, or for a long time; a whole period under consideration…Day is also put for a particular season or time when any extraordinary event happens." Many people object to the creation account of Genesis based on *their literal interpretation* of the word "day" that is used. If the "days" that were spoken of in Genesis chapter one were literal 24 hour days, then that would make the earth about 6,000 years old.

On the other hand, if the word "day" refers to a long period of time or a particular season when extraordinary events took place, then that definition would make perfect sense. I personally have no problem with the earth being older than 6,000 years. If we understand that the "days" that are spoken of in Genesis were not literal 24 hour days, then it does not matter how old the earth is. The earth could be billions of years old and still not contradict the creation account in Genesis chapter one. Colossians 1:16-18 also testifies that God (through Christ) is the Creator of all things. It states…"For by Him were all things created, that are in heaven, and that are in earth, visible and invisible, whether they be thrones, or dominions, or principalities, or powers: all things were created by Him, and for Him:

And He is before all things, and by Him all things consist. And He is the Head of the body, the church: Who is the beginning, the firstborn from the dead; that in all things He might have the preeminence."

FINAL CONCLUDING THOUGHTS

After taking a look at the facts, it is quite clear that Darwin used the proof of micro-evolution (the adaptations and changes within a species) to attempt to support his "theory" of macro-evolution (the addition of new traits or a transition to a new species). While micro-evolution is a fact, macro-evolution is not. It is only a "theory" (a proposed explanation whose status is still conjectural) at best. In other words, Darwin's "Theory" of Evolution is nothing more than his **opinion** or **theory** without sufficient evidence for proof. As I meditate on Darwin's conclusions it causes me to wonder why it is so widely accepted in the world today. The only answer that I am able to come up with is that man is always looking for a way to deny the existence of God. It seems that Darwin's "Theory" of Evolution has become a way that men and women can deny their Creator and justify it in their minds. It is for this reason that it has become a cherished work to the atheist and the agnostic. My hope for those who do not believe in God the Creator is that they will see the utter foolishness of believing that there is no God, or that life (as complex and marvelous as it is) resulted from non-life. In actuality, this is an impossibility of science and the natural world. Psalm 53:1 puts it this way…"The fool has said in his heart, There is no God." In conclusion, here are some very good reasons not to believe in Darwin's "Theory" of Evolution:

1. It is impossible to have creation without a Creator.

2. Darwin's book, The Origin of Species, gives us absolutely NO ANSWERS that actually pertain to "the origin of species."

3. The fossil record does not support Darwin's "Theory". According to *Science Digest*, "No fossil or other physical evidence directly connects man to ape."

4. Micro-evolution is a fact that is plainly observable throughout nature, but on the other hand, macro-evolution is a theory that has never been observed in science.

5. Natural selection (along with mutation) is said to have caused organisms to evolve from one basic kind (animals which can reproduce with one another) into another basic kind. This is prohibited genetically since all of the information for the development of an organism has already been encoded in the DNA of its parent. Variation to organisms must remain within its basic kind.

6. The Scriptures clearly identify God as the Creator of ALL THINGS, including the heavens, the earth realm, and all that exists within them.

7. The book of Genesis teaches us that life reproduces after its own kind. Once again, variation to organisms must remain within its basic kind.

PART 3 - OF HIM, THROUGH HIM, AND TO HIM

In light of the information we have just presented, let us go one step further as we acknowledge our God as the Creator. It will be our goal in this short teaching to examine the Scriptures in order to explain the substance (that of which a thing consists) of creation. In other words, we are asking the question…"If God is the Creator, then what did He create everything out of?" Many who have been asked this question are quick to say…"God created everything out of nothing." While this may be the first reasonable answer that comes to mind, this answer is actually incorrect. It is of the utmost importance that we understand what God created everything out of, for if we are able to discover the answer to this question, then we will be greatly aided in our understanding of God's *purpose* for the creation.

OF HIM

In order to answer the question that we have just asked (What did God create everything out of?), we must look to Romans 11:36. It states… "For of Him, and through Him, and to Him, are all things: to Whom be glory forever. Amen." **According to Dr. Harold Lovelace (<u>Read And Search God's Plan</u>): "This verse, as much or maybe more than any other verse in the Bible, gives the <u>entire picture</u> in explaining all about God and His creation. Noticing the three prepositions,** *of, through***, and** *to* **and are all related to Him (God) and all things. All things are of God, all things are through God and all things are to (returning to) God."** The Emphatic Diaglott puts it this way… "Because **out of Him**, and through Him, and for Him, are all things." Well…There is our answer. GOD CREATED EVERYTHING OUT OF HIMSELF! This can also be backed up by the terminology of Colossians 1:17, which states…"And He (speaking of God the Creator and how that He created all things through Christ) is before all things, and BY HIM ALL THINGS <u>CONSIST</u>." The word "consist" that is used in this passage speaks of the composition of the creation, or what all things are made up of. In other words, all things (that were created by God) are made up of or composed of God Himself. Everything came out of Him. This verse (Romans 11:36), along with others like it, is one of the key verses that unlocks the purpose and plan of God for His creation. This information that we have just presented is VERY EXCITING and is to be seen as EXTREMELY GOOD NEWS! It brings us out of the dark concerning God, His creation, and His ultimate goal in all things.

THROUGH HIM

The word "through" is a primary preposition denoting the channel of an act. In simple terms, to say that all things are through God, is to say that all things must pass through His process of purification before they can return to Him. It is very important that we understand the process of our salvation, for it is during this time that we are being saved spirit, soul, and body. **All things must come through the blood of the cross of Christ.** THERE IS NO OTHER WAY! As we have stated in previous teachings, it is in and through our salvation process that we "appear before God" in three distinct ways. We actually go through God's three great love feasts. Once again, they are: PASSOVER, PENTECOST, AND TABERNACLES. These three feasts correspond to the justification, sanctification, and glorification of the believer. While many may think that they can bypass the "through Him" experience, they will eventually find themselves being brought into these three great feasts of God. A careful study of the Bible will show that God has always brought His people *through* tough situations, not around them, causing the situation to be avoided or bypassed, but *through* the situation. For example, do you remember God's dealings with Israel when He delivered them out of Egyptian bondage? He delivered them out of Egypt, through the wilderness, and into the Promised Land. Well...That was a type and shadow of the full salvation process that God brings us through. We are brought out of darkness and death (Egypt), through fiery trials (the wilderness) for the purpose of maturity, and into the fullness of Christ (the Promised Land). What Good News it is to know that all (including all things) shall be brought through God's process of purification!

TO HIM

According to J. Preston Eby:

"There is no such thing in the universe as an absolutely straight line of infinite length. All straight lines will be found to be portions of immense circles. This law of circularity runs through all nature. If you were to leave planet earth traveling steadily in one direction, the day would surely come, be it in some distant age millions or billions of years hence, when you would arrive back at the precise point of departure, having completed the circuit - home again! Someone has said (a scientist) that if we were to build a telescope that could see into infinity, we would one day be looking at the back of our heads!

This great law of circularity by which all things in God's creation are seen to RETURN to the place of their BEGINNING, in its spiritual significance, is expressed in Rom. 11:36: "For FROM HIM and THROUGH HIM and TO HIM are all things - for all things originate with Him and come from Him; all things live through Him, and all things center in and tend to CONSUMMATE AND TO END IN HIM. To Him be glory forever! Amen" (Amplified). All manifestations of nature discernible to the senses confirm this law of circularity. "The sun also arises, and the sun goes down, and hastes to its place where he arose. The wind goes toward the south, and turns about unto the north; it whirls about continually, and the wind returns again *according to his circuits*. All the rivers run into the sea; yet the sea is not full; unto the place from whence the rivers come, thither they return again" (Eccl. 1:5-7)." -end quote- (The Law Of Circularity, J. Preston Eby)

Oh what a glorious day it is when we are awakened to the truth that all things will return to God. It is though we have been set free from the prison bars and shackles of the traditions and doctrines of men. God's purpose for the creation can then be seen in all of its glory. It all begins to make sense after this key element of truth is revealed to us. No longer do we have to spend long nights agonizing over the death of unsaved loved ones, wondering if God will ever receive them into His loving and corrective arms. No longer do we have to be ashamed of our "so-called" Good News, which has portrayed God as the eternal tormentor (which teaching is not true). On the contrary, we can now (with confidence and boldness) truly proclaim that GOD IS LOVE, AND THAT HIS LOVE IS **SO FIERCE** THAT HE WILL STOP AT NOTHING UNTIL HE IS ALL IN ALL (EVERYTHING TO EVERYONE)!

Many will object to what has just been stated, citing how that man's will is too strong for God to overcome, and how that man's rebellious choices will prove to be the great obstacle that will keep many from turning to God. For those who would say such a thing, do you realize what you are saying? You are saying that God is either too weak or too cruel to cause all things to return to Him. So…If all things will not return to Him, then our God is not *able* or *willing* to reconcile all things unto Himself. Surely this is not the case concerning our GREAT GOD!

Romans 11:36 is one of those **direct statements** in Scripture (along with many others) that declares the beginning, middle, and end of the purpose and plan of God. It screams from the mountaintop that God is SOVEREIGN AND ALMIGHTY, and that nothing is too difficult for Him. It tells us that not only is God *able* to bring all things unto

Himself, but that He also *desires* for all things to return to Him. If all this was not enough, this Scripture verse lines up with the very principles of science, which state…"There is no such thing in the universe as an absolutely straight line of infinite length. All straight lines will be found to be portions of immense circles." So…If all things are **of** and **through** God, **THEN IT IS _IMPOSSIBLE_ FOR ALL THINGS NOT TO <u>RETURN</u> TO GOD!** In other words, it is impossible for God to be the Creator of all things (out of Himself) and not have His creation return to Him. Sooner or later all things must return to their point of origin. What else can we possibly say on so great a subject as this? It would be fitting to close with the words of the apostle Paul, when he stated…"O the depth of the riches both of the wisdom and knowledge of God! How unsearchable are His judgments, and His ways past finding out!" (Romans 11:33)

PART 4 - SPEAKING THE TRUTH IN LOVE

Now that we have established several legitimate reasons to believe in the authenticity of the Holy Scriptures and that God is indeed the Creator, let us consider another very important point that should concern us as Christians. That which I am referring to is: **speaking the truth in love**. Notice the two parts of this phrase, which bring our attention to the fact that we are called to speak the truth, but that it also must be done in love. This statement comes from Ephesians 4:14-15, which states…"That we henceforth be no more children, tossed to and fro, and carried about with every wind of doctrine, by the sleight of men, and cunning craftiness, whereby they lie in wait to deceive; But speaking the truth in love, may grow up into Him in all things, Which is the Head, even Christ…" It is so very important for all of those who minister the Good News to understand both parts of this equation. If we fail to embrace the idea of speaking the truth in love, then we will ultimately be out of balance and extremely ineffective in our efforts to spread the Good News.

A PROPER BALANCE

All of us have known people who make it their business to speak to every person they come in contact with on a daily basis about the Lord, including strangers they have never met before in their life. They usually start out by asking the person they are talking to if they are saved, if they go to church, or they ask them if they know what will happen to them after they die. Depending on the response they receive, they move on to the next part of their formula. This usually consists of a few minutes of quoting Scriptures at the person to make them scared enough to accept the Lord on the spot. After they are finished their session of quoting Scriptures they usually feel relieved. The reason for this is because they have been taught that they will no longer have "blood on their hands" concerning that person. The person who is doing all of this "so-called" preaching never stops to realize that they come across harsh, insensitive, ignorant, and belligerent. In most cases, the result is that the person who was preached at becomes even more bitter toward the Lord and those who claim to be His followers.

The scenario just presented involves a person who may mean well, but is missing an important part of the equation necessary to effectively deliver the Gospel. A presentation of truth that is void of the love (character and nature) of God is a fleshly attempt to try to win converts based on fear, control, and manipulation. I am not saying that we should be timid when it comes to speaking the truth, BUT IT MUST BE SEASONED WITH THE LOVE THAT COMES FROM GOD! In essence, **people want to know that you care before they care what you know, or what you want them to know.** When we are witnessing to a person they are able to sense what our agenda is. If our agenda is one of fear, control, and manipulation that is motivated by our own fear of "getting blood off of our hands", then the person we are talking to will surely sense it. As well, if our agenda for sharing the Gospel is to instill fear in the listener to accept Christ in order to miss eternal torture in a never-ending hell (which teaching is not correct), then they will surely sense this also. Our speaking of the truth must be motivated by God's love for us and the person who is before us. We must have the proper balance of God's truth that is motivated by His love. To speak the truth in love means that we are not out to prove that we are right; trying to overpower our listener as though we have set our sights on winning a debate. Speaking the truth in love is just the opposite. It is the character and nature of God flowing through us that motivates us to be led by the Spirit of God and not by the flesh. It is His love that gives us the right motivation for speaking His truth. God's love brings us to the place that we are genuinely concerned for the person that we are talking to, having only his best interest in mind.

On the other hand, there are those who go about trying to love everyone they come in contact with, but they fail to speak the truth of God into the lives of these people. This type of approach is what typically characterizes the New Age Movement. This type of "so-called love" is nothing more than a warm, fuzzy, mushy, and New Age counterfeit to the true love of God. If we fail to speak the truth when given an opportunity, then we really do not understand the love of God. Remember…Jesus told us…"And <u>you shall know the truth</u>, and <u>the truth shall make you free</u> (John 8:32)." If we love those we are speaking to, then we would surely want to see them made free. What other way can they be made free, if not by knowing the truth? Those who have bought into New Age thinking tend to gravitate to the idea that every person can choose or find their own way to God. As was stated earlier, this leads to a soft, mushy, and non-direct approach of ministry, which in turn causes the listener to remain in bondage. Remember…IT IS ONLY THROUGH THE KNOWLEDGE OF THE TRUTH THAT A PERSON CAN BE MADE FREE! WE MUST SPEAK THE TRUTH! We must speak the Gospel of the Lord Jesus Christ, for **JESUS IS THE WAY, THE TRUTH, AND THE LIFE.**

GROWING UP INTO HIM

Let us now bring our attention back to Ephesians 4:15. Not only does it tell us to speak the truth in love, but it also tells us the result of speaking the truth in love. We are told that the end result is GROWTH. The latter part of verse fifteen states…"*that we* may grow up into Him in all things, Which is the Head, even Christ…" This is why it is essential for us to grasp the words of the apostle Paul in this verse. In order for a person to grow in grace and in the knowledge of the Lord they must be presented with the truth of God's Word, including the penetrating love of God. The reason so many Christians fail to grow up into Christ is due to the fact that most do not hear God's truth or understand His unconditional love. The majority of Christian teaching is nothing more than repeated rhetoric, clichés, jargon, and half-truths watered down by the traditions and doctrines of men. It is time for the Christ (Jesus and His body) to stand up in this hour and come forth with the true Gospel that is powered by the genuine love of God. Only these two things (God's truth and love) can destroy the lies of religion that hold unbelievers and believers in bondage to the carnal mind and a calloused heart that must be pierced by God's love. Remember…The goal is to "grow up into Him in all things, which is the Head, even Christ…"

There seems to be a lack of revelation within the church concerning the knowledge of Christ. Most people (including Christians) view Christ (the Anointed One) as simply a historical figure (the Son of God) that lived, died, and rose again. While all of this is true, this is not the full understanding of the meaning of Christ. If we are going to grow up into Christ, then it would be **very helpful** to understand <u>Who</u> and <u>What</u> the Christ really is. 1ˢᵗ Corinthians 12:12 is definitely one of the key Scriptures that unlocks the meaning of the Christ. It states…"For as the body is one, and has many members, and all the members of that one body, being many, are one body: ***SO ALSO IS CHRIST***." It is also interesting to note that Colossians 1:15 refers to Christ as "the image of the invisible God." While both of these statements are first and foremost referring to the Lord Jesus (the firstborn of every creature), THEY ALSO REFER TO ALL THE MEMBERS OF HIS BODY, for all the members of that one body, being many, are one body. So…It could be said that Jesus is the Head and we are His body. This is the true and full definition of the Christ. The Christ is a many membered man (body) with Jesus as the Head. It is not just Jesus alone, but it is Jesus and His body. We are one with Him, and also an extension of Him. We are the body of Christ! How could we possibly be separate from Jesus if we are His body? If a body is separated from its head, then neither the body nor the head can function.

A CALL TO MATURITY

This understanding of Christ is what must be taught as we venture forth to speak the truth in love. It is only in and through the knowledge of the Christ (that we have been called into) that we can grow up into Him. All other teachings are simply ideas from the minds of carnal men and women that cause Christians to become stunted in their growth and remain as spiritual infants. Can you imagine if every believer came to the realization that Christ is not "up in heaven somewhere", but that the Christ (the anointing, or Anointed One) IS IN THEM, THE HOPE OF GLORY (Colossians 1:27)? As well, believers must also see themselves as the **image** of the invisible God. Was this not the purpose of our Heavenly Father from the very beginning? Do you remember God's intention with man that was spoken of in Genesis 1:26? It states…"Let Us make man in Our **image**, after Our likeness…" After evaluating the words of the apostle Paul concerning God's truth and love, we are surely able to see the need for ministry, how we are to deliver God's message, and the wonderful results of the Gospel once it takes root in the heart of the believer. My hope for all who read these words is that you will continually fall in love with Jesus, being ever ready to be an ambassador and messenger of His truth and love.

PART 5 - THE KEY OF THE BOTTOMLESS PIT

According to J. Preston Eby:

"The "bottomless pit" is certainly not a hole in the ground; it is, rather, a Semitic symbol which signifies a state or condition wherein there is no bottom, thus NO GROUND TO STAND UPON. Satan was given "ground" in man's life when the Almighty declared to him, "Upon your belly shall you go, and dust shall you eat..." (Gen. 3:14). Praise God, when our adversary, the Devil, is cast into the bottomless pit, it means that he is circumvented to a realm where he has no ground to stand upon, no base for his activity, and no foundation upon which he can build his work. God is "pulling the rug out from under the Devil" as He renews our minds and transforms our nature, that there be no basis upon which the forces of evil can operate. This indicates such a transformation of being that not only are the works of the Devil destroyed in us, but also it is impossible for him to corrupt us again. Thus conformed to the image of the Son we can say with Jesus, "The prince of this world comes, and HAS NOTHING (no place) IN ME!" -end quote- (The Bottomless Pit, J. Preston Eby)

THE KEY

Revelation 20:1-3 speaks of an angel, the key of the bottomless pit, a great chain, the dragon (the serpent, the Devil, and Satan), and that he is to be bound for a thousand years. It states…"And I saw an angel come down from heaven, having the key of the bottomless pit and a great chain in his hand. And he laid hold on the dragon, that old serpent, which is the Devil, and Satan, and bound him a thousand years, And cast him into the bottomless pit, and shut him up, and set a seal upon him, that he should deceive the nations no more, till the thousand years should be fulfilled: and after that he must be loosed a little season." This passage of Scripture contains a tremendous amount of symbolism that must be rightly divided. Once we can understand the terminology that is here presented, we will become enlightened as to how that God operates. Let's take a look.

The first symbol that we will look at in this passage is the "key". I find it **fascinating** that GOD (through His angel, or messenger) IS THE ONE WHO HOLDS THE KEY AND IS IN CHARGE OF IT! The word "key" is a metaphor in the New Testament that denotes power and authority of various kinds. With this in mind, LOOK WHO IS THE ONE HOLDING THE KEY. IT IS GOD! **This proves that GOD is the One**

**in charge of deceiving the nations and He is also the One Who lifts
the sway of deception off of the nations.** He is over it all! He is the only
One capable of unlocking the door of revelation truth to us, and He is
the One Who locks the human race up in deception or disobedience
for a period of time. Listen again to what this passage is saying. It
states that there is a time for the nations to be deceived, and there is a
time for the deception to be lifted. If God is able to bring the nations
out of deception, but does not do it until the appointed time, THEN
THERE MUST BE A PURPOSE FOR THE DECEPTION! Romans
11:32 states…"For God has concluded them all (Jews and Gentiles) in
unbelief, that He might have mercy upon all." Here is the same verse
from Today's English Version. It states…"For God has made all people
prisoners of disobedience, so that He might show mercy to them all."
WHAT AN INCREDIBLE VERSE OF SCRIPTURE! That sounds like
God is the One in charge of deception to me. It also proves to us that He
is sovereign and almighty.

As was already briefly mentioned, this proves that there is a purpose
for deception. If God is sovereign, which He is, then we would have
to say that He even planned and wanted the deception of the nations
to take place. If we deny this statement, then we will have to deny
God's sovereignty. He is either in charge of everything, or He is not.
It is as simple as that. If evil, the powers of darkness, and deception
are not under His control, then we must say that God is not in control
of everything. It is quite ironic that much of Evangelical Christianity
teaches that God is sovereign, but they usually contradict themselves in
the very next breath by saying that God is supposedly fighting against
the Devil and trying His best to defeat Him. If God is fighting against
something, then He is surely not in control of it. The Scriptures, though,
tell us that He holds the key of the bottomless pit and is in charge of the
Devil and deception. So…If God is in charge of deception, what is His
purpose for bringing this upon the nations?

We must first understand that God starts everything in darkness and
then brings it into His marvelous light. As well, it is a principle of God
that something must die before it can come forth in resurrection life.
It is the principle of death, burial, and resurrection. God subjected the
creation to vanity (futility, or failure), not willingly. It is in understanding
this that we will be able to see God's purpose for deceiving the nations
(all people). As we continue to look into Romans 8:19-21 it all begins to
make sense. These two verses tell us that "God subjected the creation to
this vanity in hope, because the creation itself shall be delivered from the

bondage of corruption into the glorious liberty of the children of God." Earlier in verse nineteen Paul makes a reference to the *manifestation of the sons of God*. So…Everything is hinging on this event (the manifestation of the sons of God). Jesus, of course, was the Pattern and Type of this event. He was manifested as "The" Son of God in order to bring forth many sons in His likeness. The only reason there shall be a manifestation of the sons of God is because there was a manifestation of "The" Son of God. In essence, He was "the corn of wheat" spoken of in John 12:24 that died and was buried, including being raised from the dead, to bring forth much fruit in His image and likeness.

The whole point to see here is that deception is necessary to carry all of this out. Just as it is necessary for something to die before it can be raised from the dead, coming forth in resurrection life, it is necessary for something (the creation) to be placed into darkness (deception, or vanity) so that light (truth) can be appreciated when it is discovered. This is why God deceives the nations. He must do this in order to pull out a remnant who can appreciate the fact that they have been brought out of deception. This same remnant (according to the apostle Paul) will then be used TO DELIVER THE CREATION FROM THE BONDAGE OF CORRUPTION! The reason they will be so effective is due to the fact that they know what it is to be deceived and to be brought out of deception into the marvelous light of the Lord Jesus Christ. ISN'T THAT GLORIOUS? CAN YOU SEE IT? DON'T YOU WANT TO BE A PART OF IT? Now…Let's seek to understand what is being talked about in Revelation 20:1-3 when it refers to "the dragon, that old serpent, which is the Devil, and Satan," for this is the bondage that the creation is being delivered from.

THE DRAGON, THAT OLD SERPENT, WHICH IS THE DEVIL, AND SATAN

For the sake of review, let's take a look at the terminology in Revelation 20:2 that refers to the Devil. It refers to him as the dragon, that old serpent, which is the Devil, and Satan. The word "dragon" refers to power, magnitude, and something that has far-reaching effects. The word "serpent" speaks of something that is cunning or sly, meaning to hiss or whisper. The word "Devil" means an accuser or slanderer. Finally, the word "Satan" means an adversary, speaking of someone or something that opposes or goes against another. Now that we have given the word meanings to each of these titles pertaining to the Devil, we are now in position to paint a picture of who or what the Devil really is.

If you are under the impression (according to J. Preston Eby) "that the Devil is a hideous looking creature in a funny red suit, with cloven hoofs and a forked tail, whose chief business is to tempt and endeavor by all devious means to destroy Christians--and to preside over the alleged tortures of the departed damned (end quote)," then the statement I am about to make is going to **rattle your cage!** Let me go ahead and just lower the boom. The words "dragon", "serpent", "Devil", and "Satan" are all symbolic words that refer to *THE CARNAL MIND!* I know that I have just come against hundreds of years of the traditions and doctrines of men, which state that the Devil is a fallen angelic being that used to be called Lucifer and is now the Devil. This teaching is not correct, for the name Lucifer does not refer to the Devil, but rather, it refers to the fall of Adam in the Garden of Eden. To verify this, check Isaiah 14:12 in the Amplified Bible (Footnote 'n' informs us that Lucifer being Satan is erroneous. Lucifer comes from the Latin equivalent of PHOSPHOROS which is used of a title for Jesus in 2 Pet.1:19 and corresponds to the name 'BRIGHT AND MORNING STAR').

Ok…Now that I have your attention, give me the opportunity to drive home this all-important point. I will begin by asking a series of questions. Did not Jesus refer to Peter as Satan? Did not John say there are *many antichrists*? Did not John also say there are *many deceivers*? **Did not the apostle Paul say the "carnal mind" is enmity (a feeling or condition of hostility; hatred; ill will; animosity; antagonism) against God: for it is not subject to the law of God, neither indeed can be?** Well…I rest my case!

The sooner we can begin to see that our carnal mind (corrupt nature or mind) is the dragon, that old serpent, which is the Devil, and Satan, the sooner we can embrace the solution, which is the mind of Christ. Does not our **carnal mind** have powerfully negative and far-reaching effects? Is it not cunning or sly? Does it not accuse and slander the truth of God day and night? Is it not an adversary that goes against the character and nature of God? Well…YES, YES, YES, AND YES! Have I stretched you too far? Just hang on a little while longer, for we are going to take one more plunge into the bottomless pit of our carnal minds.

THE BOTTOMLESS PIT

According to Billy Thompson:

"The bottomless pit is the **Vanity** in (Romans 8:20). Let me explain. Vanity, according to Webster, is: excessive pride, conceit, lack of usefulness, worthlessness, something vain or futile. According to the Greek, it means: depravity, empty, profitless, idol, vain, through the idea of tentative manipulation, unsuccessful search, folly, to no purpose, to chew, gnaw.

Okay...here we go. The bottomless pit is your belief system. What you believe or eat is what you become. Adam ate the fruit from the tree of the knowledge of good and evil and he broke the LAW of GOD. We were all in Adam and we have to suffer the pain and heartache of that act. We are paying for Adam's sin. That's why JESUS came. He came to get us out of the pit of our thinking. It's called the carnal mind.

Paul said..."to be carnally minded (thinking the way the world system thinks) is death." This means you are dead to the things of God because of your interpretation of God. It is impossible to please God in the carnal mind. Until you have been begotten of God, you cannot help but believe what the carnal mind is telling you.

Back in the 80's I saw on the front page of a magazine a man that was in the middle of a desert buried in the sand with just his head sticking up. The sun was beating on top of his head and he was sweating profusely, but he thought that was going to save him. Now...this guy believed in what he was doing. My question is...Where did he get that from? I think he got it from the carnal mind. What do you think?

Now we have thousands (if not tens of thousands) of ways in the world to be saved. Some people believe that cows will save them. Where do you think they got that from? Some think the sun will save them. Some think that if they kill enough infidels, they will get 100 virgins. Some think that they are the only ones that are going to be saved because they are living for God, while all the sinners are going to hell forever because they deserve it.

Are you getting the point? Sounds like a bottomless pit to me. Exodus 21:33-34 states..."**If a man opens or digs a pit, and not cover it, and an ox or an ass fall therein; the OWNER of the pit shall make it good, and give money unto the owner of them; and the dead beast shall be his.**"

God dug a pit and did not cover it. In essence, HE allowed the serpent in the Garden. According to GOD'S LAW, the OWNER ("GOD") is responsible. That's why God sent JESUS to pay for the beast (man's nature), and the ass (man's stubbornness), and the dead beast shall be His. When God paid the price we were still dead. While we were yet in sin CHRIST died for us. He paid the wages of sin which is death. He also had a plan to bring us out of the pits of hell. I haven't heard that phrase since the 90's, but I'm going to use it anyway.

In other words, God is changing the way we see Him. We have been seeing Him through the wrong mind, which is bottomless. You can come up with anything in the carnal mind that you and I think is of God, but until you study HIS WORD you have absolutely nothing to stand on. Studying HIS WORD does not save you, but it does put a foundation under your feet. It gives you something to stand on. It's not bottomless.

I have one last point to make. It is this: Jonah prayed from the fish's belly (Jonah 2:6), and the earth with her bars was about him forever (olam: undetermined time). In Jonah's case it was three days. He saw himself in prison on the earth. The point is that he recognized where he was without God. He said…"yet have You brought "UP" my life from corruption." Jonah gets specific and says in verse eight…"they that observe "LYING VANITIES" forsake their own mercy." In other words, (according to Billy) those that eat, believe, or walk in excessive pride, emptiness, vanity, conceit, folly, manipulation, or worthlessness are in the prison of their own mind (the bottomless pit).

God is in the process of bringing every man and woman out of the bottomless pit of their carnal minds. The carnal mind has no bottom. Some will come sooner, and some will come later, but everyone will come in his own order (out of the bottomless pit)!" -end quote- (Billy Thompson)

GOD IS IN CHARGE

In summary, we are able to see that God holds the key that has locked the creation into vanity, and that God is also the One Who uses the same key to unlock the door to revelation truth. He puts us in deception, and He brings us out of deception. All of this is part of His master plan, in which He has purposed from the beginning to subject the creation to vanity in order to gather out a remnant that will in turn be used to deliver the creation from the bondage of corruption. He has placed us in a **condition** in which we have no ground to stand upon. Once again, it is called the carnal mind. It is referred to in Scripture at various times as the dragon, that old serpent, which is the Devil, and Satan. It is a bottomless pit of despair and futility from which there is no escape except by the power of the Spirit of the living God. He must deliver us from this realm of death because He is the One Who dug the pit to begin with. But rest assured. He shall deliver all men in due time, bringing us out of darkness, deception, and carnality. Remember…He is the One Who holds the key!

PART 6 - ETERNITY AND TIME

There seems to be a tremendous amount of confusion concerning a proper understanding of the *difference* between eternity and time among God's people. If you were to ask the average Christian to define eternity, just about every person that was asked would answer something like..."Eternity is time that goes on forever, or unending time." Even Webster defines "eternity" as: infinite time, a seemingly endless period of time. I am sorry to have to be the one to inform the majority of the Christian Church, as well as Webster, that our current definition of eternity could not be further from the truth. It is not correct to define eternity in relation to time, for it is a totally separate entity. Not having a proper understanding of the difference between eternity and time greatly hinders our efforts to understand the Bible and to explain its contents to others. So...It's time to clean up the mess that has been left by the established visible church concerning the true meaning of eternity, or something that is eternal.

ETERNITY EXPLAINED

In simple terms, **"eternity" is timelessness**. This is where we must begin in our quest to undo the tangled mess that has been left to us by the shallow teachings of Evangelical Christianity. Something that is eternal is to be understood apart from time. As was stated at the beginning of this teaching, eternity is not time that goes on forever, or unending time. Neither did eternity stop when time began, nor would it be correct to say that it starts when time ends. It neither starts or stops. As well, eternity is not to be viewed as time standing still or something that goes on and on forever and ever, as the King James Version states, contradicting itself. Eternity is not composed of time in any way, shape, or form. In essence, it is not to be looked at as a quantity of time, but rather, it is to be viewed as a quality or state of being. For example, GOD IS ETERNAL! Now...What do we mean by that?

When we say that God is eternal, what is it we are actually saying? Contrary to popular belief, to say God is eternal does not mean we are saying He exists forever. How many times have you heard people say...God has existed from eternity past and will continue to exist until eternity future? Well...I guess you could say that statement is partially correct. There is really no such thing as eternity *past* or *future*. There is just **eternity now**. It is not so much that God was, or will be, as much as GOD IS! This is the reason He refers to Himself as the "I AM". We know He has always existed, and that He will always exist, but the greater truth is that He always DOES EXIST. Once again, He is the GREAT I AM, not the "I was", or the "I will", but the I AM!

According to J. Preston Eby:

"Eternity simply IS. Eternity is part of the very nature and person of God. Eternity transcends beyond our knowing anything having to do with time. It is not time at all. It is just a glorious experience of BEING! Eternity simply IS, just as God simply IS. Jesus said, "Before Abraham was, I AM" (Jn. 8:58) - not "Before Abraham was, I WAS." There are not past or future tenses in eternity. There is only one eternal NOW." -end quote- (Eternity, J. Preston Eby)

After hearing information such as this, the average mind that has not considered such things begins to become enlightened to the fact that there is a difference between eternity and time. It seems to be confusing at first, but once it is realized it liberates a person, bringing them into a proper understanding of the purpose and plan of God. Once again, until we come to a revelation of the meaning of eternity, as opposed to time, we will be greatly frustrated in our efforts to understand the Bible, for the Bible primarily speaks about God's dealings with man that are to be found within the ages of time.

TIME / AGES

In order to understand the Bible and its terminology we must eventually grasp the concept of ages or time. Hebrews 1:2 states…"God has in these last days spoken unto us by His Son, Whom He has appointed heir of all things, by Whom also He made the worlds…" The word "worlds" in the King James Version is a bad translation. It would have been better to translate it "ages", for it comes from the Greek word "aion". This Scripture is actually saying that GOD FRAMED THE AGES. Alright… Now we are getting somewhere. The Greek word "aion", which means an age or period of time, is an important key that unlocks the door to an understanding of God's purpose within the ages. This same concept (of an age or ages) can be found in the Old Testament. It is represented by the Hebrew word "olam", which means a hidden or concealed amount of time. Finally, we find the Greek word "aionios" used in the New Testament to speak of something pertaining to or belonging to the ages. "Aionios" is the adjective form of the noun "aion", from which it gets its force and meaning.

According to Louis Abbott:

"In Ephesians 2:7 Paul writes, *en tois aiosin tois eperchomenois*, "in the on-coming eons." KJV: "in the ages to come;" ASV: "in the ages to come." So there are past eons, a present one, and the coming eons, at least five in all. Included in these eons are all the eonian times that are mentioned in Scripture. The adjective *aionios* comes from the noun *aion* and is defined: "pertaining to or belonging to the eons." **It is an axiom of grammar that an adjective derived from a noun cannot mean more than its parent word. It must retain the essential meaning pertaining to the noun. As it has been shown, the noun refers to limited time, which had a beginning and will have an end. The adjective, then, should not be translated by such words as "everlasting" or "eternal." The adjective cannot take on a greater meaning than the noun from which it is derived. For example, hourly, an adjective, pertains to an hour, not to a year."** -end quote- (An Analytical Study Of Words, Louis Abbott)

OLAM, AION, AND AIONIOS

A proper and unbiased study of these three words ("olam", "aion", and "aionios"); along with an understanding of the difference between eternity and time, will make you free from the idolatrous, blasphemous, and ludicrous teaching of eternal torture. Once you can see that all of God's dealings with man, including judgment, wrath, punishment, and vengeance are to be found within the ages, and are corrective in nature, you will then be able to discard the false teaching that claims God will endlessly and senselessly torment the vast majority of the human race forever and ever. Nothing could be further from the truth. You will have to do a little digging, though, to see how the true meaning of these words ("olam", "aion", and "aionios") has been hidden and misrepresented by most of the modern Bible translations and Bible study tools.

I once talked to a friend who claimed that "aionios" had to mean eternal. He based his conclusion on the fact that his brother-in-law had a master's degree in Greek and claimed it to mean eternal. Well...I don't mean to be unkind, but that is the reason we are in this mess to begin with. We place all of our confidence in human intellect, Bible College, and theology, most of which is nothing more than man's ideas, or the traditions and doctrines of men. To be brutally honest, this is the same battle Jesus faced in His day. He had to go up against all of the religious leaders, who claimed to have God all figured out, not being able to discern that The very Son of God was standing in their midst. In essence,

He was battling against those with their "so-called" master's degrees. Those Pharisees, Sadducees, and scribes must have thought..."Who is this fool? He does not have the credentials we have. There is no way he can be right." Not much has changed today. Most men and women put their stock in someone who has a degree from some type of religious institution, thinking it is impossible for such a person to be wrong. Oh how we have missed it!

Therefore, let us realize the scope of the Bible is basically confined to time, not eternity. As we stated in the beginning of this teaching, God framed the ages (time) for the very purpose of the formation of the Christ (Jesus and His body - the body of Christ). Why would God give us a Book containing many things about eternity when we are reading it in time with very little hope of understanding the eternal realm in the state we are in to begin with? Would He not rather give us a Book about the ages of time, since this is where we are presently confined?

According to J. Preston Eby:

"I am compelled to state that the Bible says very little by way of a definition of eternity because the Bible is essentially a Book of time and for time. It was written for man who lives in a temporal state and who is not yet a totally eternal being. Only as we enter that *state of being* called eternity... only as HE Who IS ETERNITY becomes "All in All" in us... only as we are spiritually metamorphosized into our eternal condition... only as eternity becomes an absolute reality to us... only then will formerly temporal beings such as we now are truly comprehend and understand eternity and things of an eternal nature." -end quote- (Eternity, J. Preston Eby)

This is the reason the Bible speaks of the "life of the ages", "punishment (correction) of the ages", and the "God of the ages". Life and God will continue beyond the ages, but punishment (correction) will not. When the last enemy is destroyed, which is death; there will be nothing left but life. ALL WILL BE MADE ALIVE IN CHRIST. EVERY MAN IN HIS OWN ORDER!

After all of this information is presented to a person they usually have one final question. It is this: How is the idea or concept of eternity or timelessness expressed in the Bible? The answer to that is very simple. Timelessness or eternity is expressed by the simple phrase "no end". Other terms such as "endless", "indissoluble", "incorruptible", and "fades not away" paint a picture of the eternal realm, or something that is permanent or unending. It is very interesting that GOD DID NOT USE SUCH WORDS IN REFERENCE TO HIS JUDGMENT, PUNISHMENT, WRATH, AND VENGEANCE. **This is undeniable evidence God never intended to punish (correct) man forever, for if He did He would have made it clear by using words that could not have been understood in any other way other than endless.**

PART 7 - THE PURPOSE OF PRAYER IN
LIGHT OF GOD'S SOVEREIGNTY

What a magnificent day it is when a person becomes enlightened to the fact that God is sovereign. The word "sovereign" speaks of indisputable power, supreme and permanent authority, and something or someone who is not controlled by outside forces. Someone who is sovereign answers to no one but themselves. The Bible does not use the word "sovereign", but it clearly contains terminology which declares the absolute sovereignty of God. Daniel 4:35 states…"And all the inhabitants of the earth are reputed as nothing: and He (God) does according to His will in the army of heaven, and among the inhabitants of the earth: and none can stay (stop or halt) His hand, or say unto Him, What are You doing?" Daniel 4:35 is telling us in basic terms…WE ARE NOTHING COMPARED TO GOD. GOD IS THE BOSS AND DOES WHATEVER HE WANTS TO DO. HE IS NOT INTERESTED IN OUR OPINIONS OR OBJECTIONS. WHEN HE PUTS SOMETHING INTO MOTION THERE IS ABSOLUTELY NOTHING THAT CAN STOP IT! NO ONE CAN CHALLENGE HIS DECISIONS OR ACTIONS! In light of all we just mentioned, a person who meditates on the things of the Lord might begin to question the need or purpose for prayer. If God is sovereign, then why even bother to pray? Do our prayers change God's mind? Should we pray? How should we pray?

YES…WE SHOULD PRAY

It is recorded in Luke 11:1 that as Jesus "was praying in a certain place, when He ceased, one of His disciples said unto Him, Lord, teach us to pray, as John also taught his disciples." Now…If the Lord did not want us to pray, then He missed a great opportunity to shoot down the whole concept of prayer, for He Himself had just come from praying, and He followed up by placing His stamp of approval on prayer by explaining to the disciples how to pray. I think it is quite safe to say (according to the Scriptures) it is Scriptural, necessary, and important to pray. With this in mind, though, it is to our benefit to understand the purpose of prayer. Too many people view prayer as a magic wand to make God give them what they want; thinking everything hinges on their ability to persuade God to do or not do certain things. GOD IS NOT TO BE TREATED AS A SPIRITUAL BELLHOP! Is it right and proper to bring all of your needs before the Lord? Yes…Of course it is. The problem, though, is that many think they can just snap their fingers, muster up enough faith, and command God to produce results pertaining to their grocery list of prayer demands. This childish view of prayer is what we must expose and uncover in order to come to an understanding of the true purpose of prayer.

THE TRUE PURPOSE OF PRAYER

Some time ago I posed this very question to (John Gavazzoni) a dear man of God I respect very much and hold in high regard. Here was his response…

According to John Gavazzoni:

"The first thing that comes to my mind in the way of a fresh approach to the place of prayer in the believer's life, is that **we need to understand prayer as an element of spiritual living that has its origin in heaven directed to earth**, and by its very nature, causing a communion, a participation in its dynamic, rather than the reverse. The distorted view that God is dependent upon our requesting Him to act in order for Him to act is part and parcel of the distortion of an essentially man-centered Christianity.

Great has been the consensus among mature saints dating back to the earliest church fathers, and certainly among Christian mystics, that prayer is essentially communion with God, a communion that includes, among other elements of response, our asking God to come to us in our need and/or the need of others. That dimension of communion is simply fitting, appropriate, in that, God as the giver of every good gift, is cultivating in us that posture of looking to Him for all our needs.

Though it requires a complete reformation of our thinking, **we must become settled and grounded in the fact that we pray BECAUSE God gives, whereas it has been assumed in pseudo-orthodoxy, that God gives because we pray**. God does respond to our requests, but our requesting has been energized by the initiation of Him sharing His heart with us, and thereby granting us communion and partnership in what He does. That's God's delight.

The administration of God does involve a sequence of interaction between God and us, and when we take the whole of Scripture's explanation of the nature of that interaction, it becomes clear that, tracing each sequence back to the original initiation, it is God Who sets things in motion and catches us up into His movement, His "work," if you will.

This principle is clearly established by St. John's insistence that "we love God because He first loved us." Certainly prayer belongs to, is an element within, the larger matter of loving God. He communicates His love to us, which sets in motion relational responses in us that have at their core, dependence, trust, confidence that such love is the source of all that is truly good and to be desired. So we pray.

I would imagine that you have found, as I and many others have, that our "prayer life" has been undergoing a most fundamental transformation since we've come to understand the absoluteness of God's sovereignty. We do look to Him in prayer, and that may take the form of outward verbalizing, but not necessarily. It may just be an inward bent of the soul toward God, an opening of the heart to His beneficent will for ourselves and others.

It may, as I've experienced, take the form of receiving an inner picture of what God is about to do, and in that, becoming instrumental in His doing by the response of agreement. I saw myself once, standing in front of a massive door, and knew that I was to push open the door, having been asked by a close brother in the Lord to pray that God would give him a door of utterance in a certain situation. I did that in my mind's eye, and the huge door was opened, not all the way, but as I intuitively understood, enough to provide that "door of utterance" opening. I had, in my mind's eye pushed at the door to open it a bit, all the while being made to understand that it was "not I, but Christ living in me."

It may simply take the form of a deep caring, an entering into the cry for help, a cry of neediness from someone, so that you are carrying their burden in your heart in the presence of the Lord. It may simply be a standing in agreement with someone that God's will be done, and that agreement supports them and encourages them to "stand fast."

Lastly, let's not forget the factor of prayer bringing us into alignment with the nature of God. Prayer is more about affecting us than affecting God. God is rightly aligned, rightly related to us. He is absolutely faithful to us and always acting toward us in the integrity of His love and grace. **Prayer gets us lined up with that reality**.

I hasten to say that prayer can often be---and it has been so in my experience of the most recent years of my walk with the Lord---simply a quiet, wordless, opening to His presence; a turning of the heart to God in such a way that words are not needed, and in fact, are not adequate to the experience." -end quote- (John Gavazzoni)

PRAYER CHANGES US, NOT GOD

How refreshing it is to know the true purpose of prayer. In summary, we are now able to see that:

1. **We need to understand prayer as an element of spiritual living that has its origin in heaven directed to earth, and by its very nature, causing a communion, a participation in its dynamic, rather than the reverse.**

2. **We must become settled and grounded in the fact that we pray BECAUSE God gives, whereas it has been assumed in pseudo-orthodoxy, that God gives because we pray.**

3. **Lastly, let's not forget the factor of prayer bringing us into alignment with the nature of God. Prayer is more about affecting us than affecting God.**

How beautiful are the words of the Lord Jesus as He taught the disciples to pray. They are enlightening and informative as to God's purpose concerning His Kingdom on this earth. Our purpose in prayer should be to line up with God's Kingdom, for this is what Jesus outlined for us in His answer to the disciples. Prayer is actually an instrument that brings us into relationship with God, whereby we learn to submit to His WILL and KINGDOM. Prayer causes us to recognize God as our Father, in that we see the greatness of His name, will, and Kingdom. It teaches us God's true intention, which is to have His Kingdom come to this earth in the hearts of men and women. During prayer we are also made aware that God is the One Who gives us our daily bread, sustaining us in and through every situation. He becomes our Shepherd. In addition to all of this, we learn to forgive others even as we have been forgiven by our Heavenly Father.

The final result of a lifestyle of prayer is that we are delivered from evil and temptation, being transformed into the very image and likeness of God. THIS IS WHY WE PRAY! We pray to know Him, experience Him, talk with Him, become like Him, be an extension of Him, come in line with Him, and to be in relationship with Him. IT IS ALL ABOUT HIM, becoming one with our Creator.

Prayer is not about commanding God to do things, but it is about having His commandments written on our hearts. When this is accomplished we will pray according to the will of our Father, being led by His Spirit, receiving the things we ask for because we have prayed according to His will, not ours. Our prayer life is what brings us into oneness and union with our Heavenly Father. This causes us to partake, participate, and operate in His divine nature. We actually become a part of what God is doing in the situations of the earth; not that we are the ones affecting each situation by our prayers, but rather, we have simply submitted to His will and Kingdom in each situation that is brought to Him in prayer.

PART 8 - HONEST ABOUT EARNEST

Have you ever come in contact with Christians that say things like..."I am not waiting on anything...or...Everything in the Bible has already been fulfilled...or...This is as good as it is going to get...or...Stop looking to the future?" While I do not side with those who base all of their Christian experience on the future alone, not seeing God at work in their lives now, neither do I side with those belonging to the other extreme that claim they have arrived now and are not waiting on anything further to take place in their Christian experience. There seems to be so much division and confusion concerning the things that were just mentioned. It is actually mind-boggling that many are not able to see the **_simplicity_** of what the Bible teaches concerning this subject matter. What are we to do? I think this is another one of those times we need to study to show ourselves approved unto God. I am confident that with a little bit of study, prayer, reasoning, and common sense we will be able to find our way out of this perplexing dilemma.

THE EARNEST OF THE SPIRIT

Alright...Let's get right to the point. 2nd Corinthians 1:22 states..."God has also sealed us, and given the **earnest** of the Spirit in our hearts." In addition to this, Romans 8:18-25 states..."For I reckon that the sufferings of this present time are not worthy to be compared with the glory which **shall** be revealed in us. For the earnest expectation of the creature **waits** for the manifestation of the sons of God. For the creature was made subject to vanity, not willingly, but by reason of Him Who has subjected the same in hope, because the creature itself also **shall** be delivered from the bondage of corruption into the glorious liberty of the children of God. For we know that the whole creation groans and travails in pain together until now. And not only they, but ourselves also, which have the **firstfruits** of the Spirit, even we ourselves groan within ourselves, **waiting** for the adoption, to wit, the redemption of our body. For we are saved by hope: but hope that is seen is not hope: for what a man sees, why does he yet hope for? But if **we hope for that we see not**, then do **we with patience wait** for it."

Within these two passages of Scripture that were just cited there are key words to help us understand the purpose and plan of God concerning the here-and-now as well as what is still yet to come at an appointed time in the future. Pay close attention to the words "earnest", "firstfruits", and "waiting". A simple understanding of these words will give us a clear picture of God's intentions concerning our relationship with Him in the here-and-now, including what it is we are still waiting for that is to come at the appointed time.

Earnest: 1. A portion of something, given or done in advance as a pledge of the remainder. 2. Anything that gives pledge, promise, or indication of what is to follow.

Firstfruits: 1. The first gathered fruits of a harvest, offered to God in gratitude. 2. The first results of an undertaking.

Waiting: 1. Assiduously (with care and persistence) and patiently waiting for something. 2. To remain or stay in expectation of; await: *wait one's turn.*

All of this terminology appears to be very simple to understand, but for the sake of those who are reading this and are not sure where they stand on the subject at hand, we will attempt to explain these Scripture passages even further, using plain and down-to-earth speech.

When 2nd Corinthians 1:22 speaks of the *earnest* of the Spirit, it means just that. We must understand that we have been given a portion or pledge of the Spirit of God in our hearts, having the promise of the fullness of the Spirit that is yet to come at the appointed time. This verse also tells us we have been sealed (to set a seal upon, mark with a seal, to seal) by the Spirit of God to receive this promise. If we are not supposed to be waiting on anything (as many in the Kingdom movement claim today), then why would the apostle Paul state in Romans 8:23 that he had the *firstfruits* (the first results of an undertaking) of the Spirit, and that he was **WAITING for the time he referred to as the adoption (the placing of a fully mature son of God), which would include the redemption of his body???** He even went on to say "we are saved by hope: but hope that is seen is not hope: for what a man sees, why does he yet hope for? **BUT IF WE HOPE FOR THAT WE SEE NOT, THEN DO WE WITH PATIENCE <u>WAIT</u> FOR IT.**"

How much more plain and simple could it be? God is at work in us now, giving us the earnest of His Spirit, but we are still waiting for the time of our adoption, in which we shall be son-placed, receiving the fullness of the Spirit which is to inhabit a new and glorified body. Paul referred to this as the redemption of our body. In simple terms, we are still waiting for God to take away the mixture we are currently being subjected to for the purpose of learning how to overcome the flesh (mortality). Let's be honest. We are still in a realm of limitation at present, but we "groan within ourselves", waiting for the time in which God will usher us into a realm with no limitations, in which even our bodies shall be redeemed, no longer being subject to mortality or corruption. Are we there yet? No. Are we in the process and on our way? Yes!

According to Dr. Stephen Jones:

"The key to understanding the Kingdom of God is to view it in its three stages of development, rather than pitting one view against another. Some say the Kingdom is NOW, and they are certainly correct. Others say the Kingdom is FUTURE, and they are correct as well. A few even say that the Kingdom of God began with Moses, and they too are correct. The Kingdom of God did indeed begin in the time of Moses when God first organized Israel into a kingdom at Horeb. But the Kingdom of God was manifested in a greater manner under a Pentecostal anointing in the second chapter of Acts.

But the Kingdom of God is also yet future as of this writing. We **await** the outpouring of the Spirit under the Feast of Tabernacles, which will manifest the Kingdom of God in its highest form on the earth. Only this view is large enough to encompass both those who believe the "Kingdom Now" idea, as well as the "Future Kingdom" viewpoint.

Under Moses, the people of Israel no doubt thought that the Kingdom of God had come in its fullness in their day. It was not revealed to them that there was much more yet to come, except in a progressive revelation of the prophets who came later. Even so, most of the people did not understand the true meaning of their own feast days. **They had focused too much upon the rituals themselves in trying to please God.** This is why they did not recognize the true Lamb of God when John pointed Him out to the people (John 1:29), nor did they see that He would have to die at Passover for the sin of the world.

The early Church understood clearly the meaning of the Feast of Passover. They wrote extensively about its fulfillment in Jesus' death. But the people were only Pentecostal in their outlook. They had moved up one level, and this had greatly increased their understanding of the plan of God. However, they had little or no understanding of the Feast of Tabernacles. Pentecost was their prime focus, and this is perfectly understandable, for it was a new and marvelous thing in the earth. To many, it was the end and goal of all history. But the revelation of Tabernacles was not clearly understood, because it was too early for this to be revealed. Kingdom people had to have opportunity to explore the marvels of Pentecost before overwhelming them with a serious revelation of Tabernacles.

So God saved the revelation of the Feast of Tabernacles for the end of the Pentecostal Age in the twentieth century. The types and shadows of Scripture seem to indicate that the Pentecostal Age was meant to last for about 40 Jubilee cycles, or 1,960 years (49 x 40). A Jubilee time cycle is 49 years. The Jubilee year was the fiftieth year, but that was also the first year of the next Jubilee cycle. God measures time in sevens, and so 40 Jubilees of time would be 1,960 years. It may be, then, that the Pentecostal Age, which began in 33 AD, began to come to a close in 1993 in preparation for a greater Age to come under the anointing of the Feast of Tabernacles." -end quote- (Creation's Jubilee, Dr. Stephen Jones)

Why is something as simple as this so hard for many of God's people to understand? Most Christians are out of balance concerning an understanding of these things. Some base everything on the future, and others base everything on the here-and-now. Both of these extreme views are incorrect. It is not all about the future, and it is not all about the here-and-now. IT IS ABOUT BOTH! The important thing for us to see now, though, is that we have the earnest of the Spirit in our hearts, waiting for the appointed time in which we shall receive the fullness of God's Spirit which is to be manifested in and through the redemption of our bodies.

Once again, Paul referred to this as the MANIFESTATION OF THE SONS OF GOD. Some claim to have already experienced this, stating they are not waiting on anything that is futuristic or yet to come in their Christian walk. **I am sorry to have to be the one to tell these people that they are caught up in a delusion of the carnal mind, which causes them to believe they can operate outside of the purpose and plan of Jesus Christ, claiming they are in no need of further sanctification or correction to be made into the image of the Son of God.** This is also defined in the Bible by the words "a worker of iniquity". The word "iniquity" means *lawlessness*. Those who do not recognize God's process of sanctification, WHICH INCLUDES WAITING, are refusing the most important part of their salvation process. They are refusing to have the spirit of the law written on their hearts. Even though they are believers, their refusal to submit to God's process of sonship places them in the category of a "worker of iniquity". In essence, they have been justified, but they are practicing lawlessness by their rejection of the sanctifying and purifying fiery trials of Almighty God.

WAITING

Not only is it Scriptural to say we are waiting on things to happen that are in the future and have not yet happened, but it is important and necessary for us to wait on God, for this is what purifies us, burning up our wood, hay, and stubble (carnality). 1st John 3:2-3 states…"Beloved, now are we the sons of God, and it does not yet appear what we shall be: but we know that, when He shall appear, we shall be like Him; for we shall see Him as He is. **AND EVERY MAN THAT HAS THIS <u>HOPE</u> IN HIM PURIFIES HIMSELF, EVEN AS HE IS PURE.**" Do you remember how Paul spoke of hope in Romans 8:24-25? He told us "we are saved by hope: but hope that is seen is not hope: for what a man sees, why does he yet hope for? But if we hope for that we see not, then do we with patience wait for it." It is also interesting to note how this passage (1st John 3:2-3) tells us that we are the sons of God NOW, but it also tells us we are HOPING AND WAITING for something greater to come. It speaks of the earnest and the fullness. How plain and simple can it be?

The reason I believe all of this information is so important is because many are out of balance concerning the things that have been stated in this teaching. On one side of the spectrum, many place all of their focus on what is to come, not realizing they are the sons of God now. On the other side of the spectrum, many place all of their emphasis on the here-and-now, not recognizing the waiting and sanctification process they are currently in. If a person will be honest with themselves and what the Scriptures actually teach, then I think these things will become clear and easy to understand. **We must drop all personal agendas** and adhere to the purpose and plan of God for us as individuals, including His purpose for the creation as a whole. It is not about trying to make every Scripture about the future, or every Scripture about right now. It is about RIGHTLY DIVIDING THE WORD OF TRUTH! The apostle Paul cleared this subject up once and for all when he stated…"Not as though I had already attained, either were already perfect: but I follow after, if that I may apprehend that for which also I am apprehended of Christ Jesus. Brethren, I count not myself to have apprehended: but this one thing I do, forgetting those things which are behind, and reaching forth unto those things which are before, I press toward the mark for the prize of the high calling of God in Christ Jesus." (Philippians 3:12-14)

PART 9 - WHY IS IT THOUGHT INCREDIBLE
THAT GOD RAISES THE DEAD?

It has come to my attention that many of those in the sonship realm (those who teach sonship and the Kingdom of God) do not believe in the resurrection of the dead. If they were questioned about it, they would say…"I believe in the resurrection, but it has already happened, and I already have it. There is no futuristic bodily resurrection of the dead." In essence, they spiritualize the resurrection of the dead in order to deny the bodily aspect of it. It is quite ironic, though, that Bill Britton, one of the fathers of the sonship movement, DID BELIEVE IN THE RESURRECTION OF THE DEAD! Regardless of whether or not you agree with all the details of how Bill Britton states the resurrection of the dead will take place, the important thing to see is that he did believe in the resurrection of the dead. None of us know all of the details pertaining to this event, but it is going to happen, and that is the important point to see. Here is a quote from Bill Britton about this very subject.

According to Bill Britton:

"I have refuted against these fellows for years who claim there isn't going to be a resurrection. They spiritualize the resurrection and say that these bodies are just going to go to dust and that's the end of it. But this is not true. Jesus Christ is coming and we are looking for Him and He shall appear to change these bodies of our humiliation and make them like unto His body of glory! No where does the Bible indicate that these bodies will disintegrate or go back to dust. God is saving every bit of the molecules, the automical structure, whether you cremate it, whether it's destroyed to our sense of seeing, or whatever happens to it, God never loses track of the substance. He still knows where it is. He is going to take those which once were the bodies we walked in for those who went on and He's going to bring them back. Out of those who have been sown in the earth, He's going to bring forth a harvest of a body of His glory!

This body of His glory is going to be far greater than the body we are now in, because the body is coming out by the resurrection power and glory of God. Whether you come through the grave or by the change that Paul talks about, it's still resurrection life that changes our bodies. Even if you don't go to the grave, it's going to be His resurrection power that brings you through the change. And it's going to be the resurrection power that brings the bodies out of the grave. As a result, this resurrection life that changes this physical body doesn't bring back just the same thing that went in the grave. Paul says that when we sow grain, what we expect is far greater than what we sowed, isn't it? He said that's the same way it is in the resurrection. What is sown in corruption is going to be brought forth in incorruption and is therefore a far greater harvest than what was sown. What am I saying? Starting with the body, I am saying that the bodies we come into by the resurrection life of Christ are going to be so far superior. These bodies will be far beyond in their glory and ability extending farther than this body we are now in, that there will hardly be any comparison. In fact, Paul says that he reckoned the sufferings of this present time in this body are not even worthy to be compared with the glory that's going to be revealed in us. It is difficult to compare the glory of that resurrection body with the body that we now have." -end quote- (Spirit, Soul, and Body, Bill Britton)

Well…That sure lets us know where Brother Bill Britton stood on the issue of resurrection. Not only did Bill Britton believe in the resurrection, but so did Job, Isaiah, Daniel, Hosea, John, Jesus, and Paul. That sounds like some pretty good company to me. If Job, Isaiah, Daniel, Hosea, John, **Jesus**, and Paul believed and taught the resurrection of the dead, then you would have to admit this gives CREDIBILITY to the teaching which states that God raises the dead. In other words, the very fact that these men of God taught the resurrection of the dead tells us we can believe and trust in the hope that God is willing and able to raise the dead, bringing them into a state of incorruption and immortality for the purpose of ruling the nations during the Tabernacles Age. It also tells us there shall be a second general resurrection of the just and unjust for the purpose of restoration and correction. This truth has been established in the mouths of two or more witnesses. Let's take a moment to hear from these men who have testified down through history concerning the resurrection of the dead.

JOB, ISAIAH, DANIEL, HOSEA, JOHN, JESUS, AND PAUL

According to Job:

"For I know that my Redeemer lives, and that He shall stand at the latter day upon the earth: **And though after my skin worms destroy this body, YET IN MY FLESH SHALL I SEE GOD…**" (Job 19:25-26)

According to Isaiah:

"Dead men shall live, together with **my dead body shall** they **arise**. Awake and sing, you that dwell in dust: for your dew is as the dew of herbs, and **the earth shall cast out the dead**." (Isaiah 26:19)

According to <u>Daniel</u>:

"**And many of them that sleep in the dust of the earth shall awake,** some to everlasting life (the life of the ages), and some to shame and everlasting contempt (the abhorrence or abomination of the ages)." (Daniel 12:2)

According to <u>Hosea</u>:

"**I will ransom them from the power of the grave**; I will redeem them from death: O death, I will be your plagues; O grave, I will be your destruction: repentance shall be hid from My eyes." (Hosea 13:14)

According to <u>John</u>:

"And I saw thrones, and they sat upon them, and judgment was given unto them: and I saw the souls of them that were beheaded for the witness of Jesus, and for the word of God, and which had not worshipped the beast, neither his image, neither had received his mark upon their foreheads, or in their hands; and they lived and reigned with Christ a thousand years. But the rest of the dead lived not again until the thousand years were finished. This is **the first resurrection**. Blessed and holy is he that has part in **the first resurrection**: on such the second death has no power, but they shall be priests of God and of Christ, and shall reign with Him a thousand years." (Revelation 20:4-6)

According to <u>Jesus</u>:

"And Jesus answering said unto them, Do you not therefore err, because you know not the scriptures, neither the power of God? For **when they shall rise from the dead**, they neither marry, nor are given in marriage; but are as the angels which are in heaven." (Mark 12:24-25)

"Marvel not at this: for the hour is coming, in the which **all that are in the graves shall hear His voice, And shall come forth**; they that have done good, unto **the resurrection of life**; and they that have done evil, unto **the resurrection of damnation (judgment)**." (John 5:28-29)

"And this is the Father's will which has sent Me, that of all which He has given Me I should lose nothing, but should **raise it up again at the last day**. And this is the will of Him that sent Me, that every one which sees the Son, and believes on Him, may have everlasting life: and **I will raise him up at the last day**…No man can come to Me, except the Father which has sent Me draw him: and **I will raise him up at the last day**." (John 6:39-40, 44)

According to <u>Paul</u>:

"And when they heard of **the resurrection of the dead (ones – plural)**, some mocked: and others said, We will hear you again of this matter." (Acts 17:32)

"But when Paul perceived that the one part were Sadducees, and the other Pharisees, he cried out in the council, Men and brethren, I am a Pharisee, the son of a Pharisee: **of the hope and resurrection of the dead I am called in question.** And when he had so said, **there arose a dissension** between the Pharisees and the Sadducees: and the multitude was divided. **For the Sadducees say that there is no resurrection**, neither angel, nor spirit: but the Pharisees confess both." (Acts 23:6-8)

"And have hope toward God, which they themselves also allow, that **there shall be a resurrection of the dead, both of the just and unjust.**" (Acts 24:15)

"Why should it be thought a thing incredible with you, that **God should raise the dead?**" (Acts 26:8)

"And not only they, but ourselves also, which have the firstfruits of the Spirit, even we ourselves groan within ourselves, waiting for the adoption, to wit, **the redemption of our body.**" (Romans 8:23)

"Now if **Christ** be preached that He **rose from the dead, how say some among you that there is no resurrection of the dead?** But if there be no resurrection of the dead, then is Christ not risen: And if Christ be not risen, then is our preaching vain, and your faith is also vain. Yes, and we are found false witnesses of God; because we have testified of God that He raised up Christ: Whom He raised not up, if so be that the dead rise not. **For if the dead rise not, then is not Christ raised:** And if Christ be not raised, your faith is vain; you are yet in your sins. Then they also which are fallen asleep in Christ are perished. If in this life only we have hope in Christ, we are of all men most miserable." (1st Corinthians 15:12-19)

"If by any means I might attain unto **the resurrection of the dead... Who shall change our vile body, that it may be fashioned like unto His glorious body,** according to the working whereby He is able even to subdue all things unto Himself." (Philippians 3:11, 21)

"For the Lord Himself shall descend from heaven with a shout, with the voice of the archangel, and with the trump of God: and **the dead**

in Christ shall rise first: Then we which are alive and remain shall be caught up together with them in the clouds, to meet the Lord in the air: and so shall we ever be with the Lord." (1st Thessalonians 4:16-17)

"Women received their dead raised to life again: and others were tortured, not accepting deliverance; **that they might obtain a better resurrection…**" (Hebrews 11:35)

THE GREEKS, SADDUCEES, AND GNOSTICS

In light of all we have mentioned so far in this teaching, you would think that those who deny the bodily resurrection of the dead would begin to see the light. Unfortunately, many remain unmoved by the information that was just presented. Why is this? The reason for this is due to the fact that many have been influenced by the Greeks, Sadducees, and Gnostics.

According to Wayne Jackson:

"The ancient **Greeks** disdained the notion that the body could ever be raised. Thus when Paul spoke concerning "the resurrection of the dead [ones—plural]" in Athens, his message was mocked (Acts 17:32). During the time of Jesus, the **Sadducees** denied the resurrection of the body (Matt. 22:23; Acts 23:6-8).

Even some Christians in the primitive church had fallen for this error and so affirmed: "There is no resurrection of the dead" (1 Cor. 15:12)—a heresy which Paul attempted to correct. In the late decades of the apostolic age, a sect known as the **Gnostics** arose, denying the resurrection of the body." -end quote- (Growing Doubts About The Resurrection Of The Dead, Wayne Jackson)

In simple terms, those who deny the bodily resurrection of the dead have bought into the Greek worldview, especially the Greek view of matter and spirit. After taking a closer look, we will see that **the spiritualizing of resurrection has its roots in the Greek worldview, while the idea of the bodily resurrection has its roots in the Hebrew worldview.**

According to Dr. Stephen Jones:

"**Matter was not created evil.** God created all things and then pronounced it "very good" (Gen. 1:31). This is how God views creation, which establishes the foundation for the plan of God for the earth. Any view that deviates from this foundation, teaching that matter is inherently evil, is teaching from a Greek perspective, not from a Biblical, Hebraic perspective. Unfortunately, once the early Church was scattered by persecution into the Greek-speaking culture and philosophy, it did not take long for the Church to forget the Hebraic view of creation. This affected many Church doctrines and is with us yet today.

The Greek philosophers taught that spirit was good, and matter was evil. They taught that the body was a prison for the "spiritual soul," and that the only means of escaping the evil of this physical existence was for the flesh to die, so that the spiritual soul might be free. This disparaging view of matter caused some to teach that Christ, the Word (Logos) did NOT really come in the flesh, for how could a good God ever come into contact with evil matter and remain untainted by it?

Consequently, John addressed this view in the first part of his gospel and again in his letters. He says very specifically, "and the Word was made flesh" (John 1:14) and that any man who denied that Jesus Christ was come in the flesh was "not of God" (John 4:3), but of that "antichrist" spirit.

The purpose of God has always been to manifest Himself in the physical creation, so that He receives glory not only in the spiritual dimension (the heavens) but also in matter. The goal is for God's Kingdom to come to earth, and for God's will to be done "in earth as it is in heaven" (Matt. 6:10). The crescendo of this goal is for God to manifest Himself in man, who was created of the dust of the ground, whose name (Adam) means "earthly."

Man is a microcosm of the earth itself, a **little earth**. It is God's purpose to manifest Himself in man specifically, and in the earth in general. This is why He seeks to pour out His Spirit upon "all flesh" (Joel 2:28). It is the beginning of this manifestation of God in the earth *in matter*. The ultimate purpose for the resurrection of the dead is to prepare a body that is fit for the fullness of God's Spirit to indwell." -end quote- (The Purpose Of Resurrection, Dr. Stephen Jones)

As a result of the negative influence of the Greeks, Sadducees, and Gnostics, many Christians have been seduced into either spiritualizing the resurrection, saying it is already past, or redefining resurrection in terms of an awakening in the spirit or soul. Neither of these views are correct, for each one of the views just mentioned denies the bodily aspect of resurrection, which is the whole purpose of resurrection. **Do you remember when Paul had to rebuke Hymenaeus and Philetus**

for saying the resurrection was past already (2ⁿᵈ Timothy 2:17-18)? He said their word will eat as does a canker, and that they were overthrowing the faith of some. It sounds like Paul was very serious about protecting the proper teaching of the resurrection of the dead.

In order to further clarify and support the idea of the bodily resurrection of the dead, we will look at the Greek word "anastasis" (translated resurrection) and how it is used in Scripture. It is common knowledge that one of the easiest ways to find out what a word means is to look at the way it is used. In essence, the way a word is used determines what it means. As a matter of fact, it could be said that **usage determines meaning**.

"ANASTASIS"

The Christian experience is all about being brought out of death and into the life of the Son of God. What causes many to misunderstand the word "resurrection" is that they try to apply it to the spirit or soul of man, rather than realizing that the word "resurrection" pertains to the redemption of our body. While it is true that we have passed from death to life by believing on the Lord Jesus Christ, this is not the resurrection. The key to understanding how to rightly divide the Scriptures concerning man's salvation process is to understand that we are spirit, soul, and body, and that we are being saved spirit, soul, and body. The spirit must be justified, the soul sanctified, and the body glorified. It is right and proper to say we have been raised with Jesus in newness of life, and that we are seated with Him in heavenly places now, but once again, this is not the resurrection or the redemption of our body. That is still yet to come at the appointed time. It is this mixing of justification, sanctification, and glorification that causes many believers to not rightly divide the Word of truth when it comes to resurrection.

According to Dr. Stephen Jones:

"The Scriptures do tell us that through faith we move from death into life. However, the actual word "resurrection" (Gr. *anastasis*) is never used to describe the process by which one becomes a Christian. Every passage clearly speaks of resurrection in a literal sense, where those who have died rise to stand upon the earth." -end quote- (The Purpose Of Resurrection, Dr. Stephen Jones)

There are also those who try to take the Greek word "exanastasis", which means *out-resurrection from among the dead*, and say that Paul was referring to us trying to walk out the resurrection life of the Lord

Jesus. While it may not be too harmful to the Scriptures to get a spiritual application out of this passage, this is clearly not what Paul was talking about. He was referring to the first resurrection (a better resurrection), in which the overcomers shall come forth first *out from among the rest of the dead*. Go back and take a look at Philippians chapter three, reading the whole chapter and seeing how Paul ends the passage by saying that "GOD SHALL CHANGE OUR VILE BODY, THAT IT MAY BE FASHIONED LIKE UNTO HIS GLORIOUS BODY..." When Paul spoke of the resurrection and out-resurrection in this passage he was clearly referring to the bodily aspect of the resurrection of the dead.

According to Dr. Stephen Jones:

"That I may know Him [Christ], and the power of His resurrection and the fellowship of His sufferings, being conformed to His death; in order that I may attain to the resurrection from the dead [Greek: exanastasis ek nekron]."

Dr. Bullinger comments on this passage in his marginal notes in The Companion Bible. He tells us that the Greek word "exanastasis ek nekron" means OUT-RESURRECTION FROM AMONG THE DEAD. He says that the normal term used is simply "anastasis nekron," which is the resurrection of the dead--meaning all of the dead. But "EXanastasis EK nekron," he says, "implies the resurrection of some, the former of these two classes, the others behind left behind."

In other words, Paul was telling the Philippian Church that his desire was to attain the FIRST resurrection--the limited resurrection out from among the rest of the dead. Paul had no doubt that he would be resurrected. But he knew of a "better resurrection" (Heb. 11:35) that would occur 1,000 years before the general resurrection (Rev. 20:5). Paul did not doubt his salvation, but he did express concern that he might not attain this resurrection out from among the dead. Thus he continues in Phil. 3:12, saying,

"NOT THAT I HAVE ALREADY OBTAINED IT, or have already become perfect, but I press on in order that I may lay hold of that for which also I was laid hold of by Christ Jesus."

What is "it" that he had not yet obtained? He had certainly already qualified for the general resurrection as a citizen of the Kingdom. But he knew that "enduring to the end" was required to inherit the first resurrection and to rule with Christ during the thousand years of the

Tabernacles Age." -end quote- (Moses' Two Trumpets In Prophecy, Dr. Stephen Jones)

1st CORINTHIANS CHAPTER 15

How anyone could read 1st Corinthians chapter fifteen and say there is no resurrection of the dead has to be one of the most mind-boggling mysteries of all time. The entire passage (58 verses) is devoted to the topic of the resurrection of the dead. We can be certain that Paul addressed this topic to the church at Corinth due to the fact they had no doubt been heavily influenced by the Greek worldview, which claims there is no bodily resurrection of the dead. Paul passionately and persuasively states his case for the bodily resurrection of the Lord Jesus Christ and then goes on to say that His resurrection is the guarantee and pattern for our resurrection as well. How much more plain and simple could it be? Paul goes on to say in verses 12-14...**"Now if Christ be preached that He rose from the dead, how say some among you that there is no resurrection of the dead? But if there be no resurrection of the dead, then is Christ not risen: And if Christ be not risen, then is our preaching vain, and your faith is also vain."**

If we follow the path of Paul's logic, then we can clearly see he links the resurrection of the dead in general to the resurrection of the Lord Himself. If there is no bodily resurrection of the dead that is to come, then Christ Himself was not raised bodily from the tomb. To deny one is to deny the other. It is just that simple. As a matter of fact, to deny the resurrection of the dead (whether for Jesus or the dead in general) is to deny Christianity all together. If you take away the teaching and reality of resurrection, then your faith is vain, and you are still in your sins.

HOW ARE THE DEAD RAISED UP / THE NATURE OF THE RESURRECTED BODY

Many would ask the question...How are the dead raised up, and with what body do they come? Well...Paul addressed this very question in 1st Corinthians 15:35-54. He told us that the resurrected body would not be a natural body, but a spiritual body that is far greater than what we currently have now. Paul refers to it as corruption putting on incorruption, and mortality putting on immortality. Our natural body is sown in dishonor and raised in glory. It is sown in weakness and raised in power. While there is much we are not able to understand about this event, for it is beyond what we can currently grasp at present in this body, we do have the resurrection of the Lord Jesus Himself to look at, for remember…His resurrection is the guarantee and pattern for our resurrection. Let's take a look at what the Scriptures say about the resurrection of Jesus, for this will help us to gain some understanding of how the dead are raised and what the nature of the resurrected body will be like.

Luke 24:36-43 states…"And as they spoke, Jesus Himself stood in the midst of them, and said unto them, Peace be unto you. But they were terrified and affrighted, and supposed that they had seen a spirit. And He said unto them, Why are you troubled? and why do thoughts arise in your hearts? Behold My hands and My feet, that it is I Myself: handle Me, and see; for a spirit has not flesh and bones, as you see Me have. And when He had spoken, He showed them His hands and His feet. And while they yet believed not for joy, and wondered, He said unto them, Have you here any meat? And they gave Him a piece of a broiled fish, and of an honeycomb. And He took it, and did eat before them."

There are some key words in this passage to help us understand the nature of the resurrected body. They are…"But they were terrified and affrighted, **and supposed that they had seen a spirit**. And He said unto them, Why are you troubled? and why do thoughts arise in your hearts? **Behold My hands and My feet, that it is I Myself: handle Me, and see; for a spirit has not flesh and bones, as you see Me have**."

According to Dr. Stephen Jones:

"The only real question is "with what body do they come?" (1 Cor. 15:35?) Is the resurrected body physical or spiritual? The answer is: **BOTH**. He had a heavenly Father and an earthly mother, and the resurrected body was the culmination of that relationship. He could enter the spiritual dimension ("heaven") or the physical, earthly dimension at will. His Father had given Him all authority in BOTH realms, even as He said in Matt. 28:18 (NASB),

> [18] **. . . All authority has been given to Me in heaven and on earth.**

As a result, He could take a physical form where the disciples could touch Him and see the wounds of His crucifixion (John 20:27). He could also eat food with the disciples (John 21:13; Luke 24:43). Then He could vanish (Luke 24:31) just as suddenly by taking spirit form. The question of whether Jesus was merely a spirit or if He had physical characteristics is faced and answered squarely in Luke 24:36-43.

³⁶ And while they [disciples] were telling these things, He Himself stood in their midst. ³⁷ But they were startled and frightened and thought that they were seeing a spirit. ³⁸ And He said to them, Why are you troubled, and why do doubts arise in your hearts? ³⁹ See My hands and My feet, that it is I Myself; touch Me, and see, <u>for a spirit does not have flesh and bones, as you see that I have</u>. ⁴⁰ And when He had said this, He showed them His hands and His feet. ⁴¹ And while they still could not believe it for joy and were marveling, He said to them, Have you anything here to eat? ⁴² And they gave Him a piece of a broiled fish; ⁴³ and He took it <u>and ate</u> it before them.

Jesus went out of His way to prove to them that He was not a spirit and that He had "flesh and bones." He showed the disciples His physical scars, which no spirit would have. Then He asked for something to eat. A spirit cannot eat physical food.

Most commentators point out the fact that Jesus said nothing about having <u>blood</u>. He only spoke of "flesh and bones." While this is certainly true, the greater truth that He was raised with a <u>physical body</u> is often overlooked. And yet this is Luke's prime focus in the passage above, because it was the main truth that Jesus was revealing to the disciples at that moment.

This is not to say that Jesus was <u>limited</u> by His flesh to the physical world. The marvel of the moment was that Jesus, though physical, could move just as freely in the spiritual dimension as well. He was not confined to the spirit world, nor was He limited to the physical world. He had free access to both, because, as we have already pointed out, He had all authority in both heaven and earth, the spiritual and the physical realms." -end quote- (<u>The Purpose Of Resurrection</u>, Dr. Stephen Jones)

DO YOU FIND IT IMPOSSIBLE TO BELIEVE THAT GOD RAISES THE DEAD?

When the apostle Paul stood before King Agrippa to defend his beliefs it is recorded that he asked him a very important question. The question was…"Why should it be thought a thing incredible with you, that God should raise the dead?" (Acts 26:8) After everything that has been presented in this teaching I personally believe that it will be very difficult for those who deny the resurrection of the dead to continue in that vein of thinking. However, some find it hard to believe that God is able to raise the dead, and others find it hard to believe that God would want to raise the dead. In both cases it appears that <u>unbelief</u> is the root cause which stops many from believing in the resurrection of the dead. The bottom line question we must ask ourselves is this…**Did God raise Jesus from the dead?** If He did (which He did), then it stands to reason that there will be a resurrection of the dead in general (the overcomers coming forth in the first resurrection, and the rest of the dead in the general [second] resurrection). Let's ask another question. Was it hard for God to raise Jesus from the dead? The answer to that would be… NO! Well…Will it be hard for God to raise the rest of the dead? You guessed it…The answer to that question is also…NO! There is nothing too hard for the Lord!

The most important thing to see in this teaching is that the Scriptures teach the bodily resurrection of the dead. Since this is the case, then we should gladly embrace this teaching and passionately declare it to the extent the apostle Paul did. Despite the fact that even Paul did not know all of the details surrounding the resurrection of the dead, he taught it everywhere he went. He considered it so important that he said to deny the resurrection of the dead in general was to deny the resurrection of our Lord and Savior Jesus Christ. This is not a side issue in the grand scheme of things, but it is THE CENTRAL ISSUE OF CHRISTIANITY. Without resurrection there is no deliverance from sin, carnality, and mortality. "If the dead rise not, then let us eat and drink; for tomorrow we die." (1st Corinthians 15:32)

PART 10 - THE PRECIOUS BLOOD OF CHRIST

The Blood Will Never Lose Its Power
Words and Music by Andre Crouch

The blood that Jesus shed for me
Way back on Calvary
The blood that gives me strength
From day to day
It will never lose its power.

It reaches to the highest mountain
And it flows to the lowest valley
The blood that gives me strength
From day to day
It will never lose its power.

It soothes my doubts and calms my fears
And it dries all my tears
The blood that gives me strength
From day to day
It will never lose its power.

It reaches to the highest mountain
And it flows to the lowest valley
The blood that gives me strength
From day to day
It will never lose its power.

It reaches to the highest mountain
And it flows to the lowest valley
The blood that gives me strength
From day to day
It will never lose
It will never lose
It will never lose its power

THE NEW AGE MOVEMENT

The negative influence of the New Age Movement seems to gain more ground every day. Some of the leading selling New Age books are making comments like…

"There is no sin …"

A "slain Christ has no meaning."

"The journey to the cross should be the last useless journey."

"Do not make the pathetic error of clinging to the old rugged cross."

"The Name of Jesus Christ as such is but a symbol… It is a symbol that is safely used as a replacement for the many names of all the gods to which you pray."

"The recognition of God is the recognition of yourself."

"The Atonement is the final lesson he [man] need learn, for it teaches him that, never having sinned, he has no need of salvation."

According to John Gavazzoni:

"Jesus Christ is being reinvented, redefined, and blasphemed and, this false New Age Christ teaching is about to make huge inroads into the world." -end quote- (John Gavazzoni)

There have always been those who have spoken out against the blood of the cross of Christ, mocking the atonement and the price Jesus paid for the sin of the world, but it appears we are on the verge of a New Age onslaught like never before. It is for this reason we must understand the importance of the precious blood of Christ. Oh what a price that was paid to ransom the souls of men! What a sacrifice! What a loving Savior! What PRECIOUS BLOOD that was poured out for you and me!

THE LIFE IS IN THE BLOOD

Leviticus 17:11 tells us the life of the flesh is in the blood. It states…"For the life of the flesh is in the blood: and I have given it to you upon the altar to make an atonement for your souls: for it is the blood that makes an atonement for the soul." The word "life" in this passage comes from the Hebrew word "nephesh", which means "soul". So as we can see, the

Scriptures identify the blood with the soul. It is also interesting to point out at this time how the Scriptures identify our breath with our spirit and our body with the flesh. Spirit, soul, and body are represented in the Scriptures by our breath, blood, and flesh.

God instituted animal sacrifices (with the shedding of blood) in the Old Testament for the purpose of atoning for sin. We are told in the book of Exodus (chapter 12) how the Jews were instructed by Moses to take a lamb without blemish and to kill it in the evening. They were then to take the blood and strike it on the two side posts and on the upper door post of the houses they were in. After that they were to eat the flesh that had been roasted in fire along with unleavened bread and bitter herbs. This was all for the purpose of acquiring protection from the death angel that was to pass through the land, taking the lives of all the firstborn. They were told…"And the blood shall be to you for a token upon the houses where you are: AND WHEN I SEE THE BLOOD, I WILL PASS OVER YOU…"

Many people have a hard time understanding why God would do this and some even find it offensive. The important thing to see, though, is that all of the blood sacrifices in the Old Testament were mere shadows and types of THE BLOOD SACRIFICE OF THE LORD JESUS CHRIST that took place on Mount Calvary so long ago. They all pointed to **the sacrifice** of the Lord Jesus, shedding His blood on the cross to atone for and take away the sin of the world.

THE BLOOD OF THE CROSS OF CHRIST

According to Dr. Stephen Jones:

"The prime example of the manifestation of the love of God is found in Jesus Christ Himself. He did not come to consume or devour us but to give His life for the world.

The blood was to be poured out upon the ground as atonement for our souls (Leviticus 17:13). In pouring out the blood, it was said that the SOUL was poured out. This is what Jesus did at the Cross, for we read in Isaiah 53:12, "He has poured out His soul unto death." It was done by means of the blood that was poured out upon the ground at the Cross.

To pour the blood of any sacrifice upon the ground (including the Sacrifice of Christ) was an act of giving. Christ did this in accordance with the law, which said that the blood was to be used to atone for our souls." -end quote- (The Laws Of Blood And Redemption, Dr. Stephen Jones)

The blood sacrifice of the Lord Jesus Christ was THE FOCAL POINT of time (whether past, present, or future) as we know it. It was the point at which all the elements and aspects of the Old Testament (concerning the types and shadows of the coming Redeemer) came to fruition. Every animal sacrifice in the Old Testament pointed to THE SACRIFICE OF THE LAMB OF GOD (THE LORD JESUS) that would take away the sin of the world. Once again, the blood sacrifices of the Old Testament were meant to point to the blood of Jesus, which was shed to TAKE AWAY the sin of the world, for it was not possible for the blood of animals (bulls and goats) to take away our sin (Hebrews 10:4), but only to cover and atone for sin "on credit" until the time of the coming of the Messiah Who would pour out His blood for all. This is why the apostle Paul said in Hebrews 9:22 that…"And almost all things are by the law purged with blood; **and without shedding of blood is no remission (forgiveness of sin)."** Remember…This corresponds directly with the law of God concerning blood that was quoted earlier from Leviticus 17:11. Jesus had to shed His blood according to the law of God to make atonement for our souls. It was the only way!

The apostle Paul goes into great detail concerning the blood of Christ in the book of Hebrews. Here is a passage (Hebrews 9:11-15) which brings even more clarity to the subject…"But Christ being come a High Priest of good things to come, by a greater and more perfect tabernacle, not made with hands, that is to say, not of this building; Neither by the blood of goats and calves, but by His own blood He entered in once into the holy place, having obtained eternal redemption for us. For if the blood of bulls and of goats, and the ashes of a heifer sprinkling the unclean, sanctifies to the purifying of the flesh: How much more shall the blood of Christ, Who through the eternal Spirit offered Himself without spot to God, purge your conscience from dead works to serve the living God? And for this cause He is the Mediator of the New Testament, that by means of death, for the redemption of the transgressions that were under the first testament, they which are called might receive the promise of eternal inheritance."

In closing, I would like to present one more passage of Scripture that magnifies the blood of the cross of Christ. It is Colossians 1:16-20. It states…"For by Him were all things created, that are in heaven, and that are in earth, visible and invisible, whether they be thrones, or dominions, or principalities, or powers: all things were created by Him, and for Him: And He is before all things, and by Him all things consist. And He is the Head of the body, the church: Who is the beginning, the firstborn from the dead; that in all things He might have the preeminence. For it pleased the Father that in Him should all fullness dwell; **And, having made peace through** the blood **of** His **cross, by Him** *to reconcile all things unto Himself;* **by Him, I say, whether they be things in earth, or things in heaven."**

This passage of Scripture is no doubt ONE OF THE MOST **POWERFUL** passages of Scripture that was ever penned (through the apostle Paul) by the inspiration of the Holy Spirit. It declares that Jesus Christ created ALL THINGS, including things for us to wrestle against for the purpose of learning how to overcome through Him. It then goes on to declare Jesus as the Head of HIS GLORIOUS BODY – THE BODY OF CHRIST, in which all the fullness of God is to be demonstrated and manifested, bringing deliverance to a world that is held captive by futility, failure, frustration, and iniquity. The passage is **CLIMAXED** by the mention of the **marvelous** and **magnificent** "blood of the cross of Christ", which is said to have its final triumph brought about by *A RECONCILIATION OF ALL THINGS UNTO HIMSELF*. This "reconciliation of all things" is a direct result of the blood of the cross of Christ. Now…That is love and power without limit!!! The sons of God shall be manifested in the earth at the appointed time, playing a part in the reconciliation of all things in heaven and earth. Once again, this is only because there was a manifestation of THE SON OF GOD, in that He shed **His precious blood**, laying down His life for all.

What else can we possibly say concerning so great a salvation and sacrifice? It is of the utmost importance that we recognize (along with the apostle Peter) that…"We were not redeemed with corruptible things, as silver and gold, from our vain conversation received by tradition from our fathers; But with **the precious blood of Christ**, as of a Lamb without blemish and without spot: Who verily was foreordained before the foundation of the world, but was manifest in these last times for us, Who by Him do believe in God, that raised Him up from the dead, and gave Him glory; that our faith and hope might be in God." (1st Peter 1:18-21)

PART 11 - EARS TO HEAR

"The apostle John, our brother and companion in tribulation, and in the Kingdom and patience of Jesus Christ, was in the isle that is called Patmos, for the Word of God, and for the testimony of Jesus Christ. He was in the Spirit on the Lord's day, and heard behind him a great voice, as of a trumpet, saying, I am Alpha and Omega, the first and the last: and, what you see, write in a book, and send it unto the seven churches which are in Asia; unto Ephesus, and unto Smyrna, and unto Pergamos, and unto Thyatira, and unto Sardis, and unto Philadelphia, and unto Laodicea." (Revelation 1:9-11)

As John turned to see the voice that spoke to him he saw a glorious vision of the Lord Jesus Christ. It was so powerful that it caused him to fall down at His feet as though he were dead. What John was actually seeing was a vision of the complete and perfect body of Christ with the Lord Jesus as the Head. It was all too much to take in, causing John to collapse at the feet of the world's Redeemer. Jesus laid His right hand on John, saying, "fear not; I am the first and the last: I am He that lives, and was dead; and, behold, I am alive forevermore, Amen; and have the keys of hell (Hades – the grave) and of death. Jesus then told John to write the things which he had seen, and the things which are, and the things which shall be hereafter..." (Revelation 1:17-19)

John was given a message to give to the angels (messengers) of each one of the seven churches. The messages pertained to those specific churches in that day, but they also have within them prophetic value concerning the condition of the church (in general) for us today. The messages to the seven churches are both history AND prophecy. They show the progression of the church from the days of the apostles until now. Jesus addressed different issues in each message, but there is one particular statement which He made to all seven churches. Now...When Jesus says something one time it is **important!** When He says something two times it is **VERY IMPORTANT!!** But when He says something <u>seven times</u> it is <u>**EXTREMELY IMPORTANT!!!**</u> What was it that He said to all seven churches? I think it will be worth our time to find out.

HE THAT HAS AN EAR, LET HIM HEAR

"HE THAT HAS AN EAR, LET HIM HEAR WHAT THE SPIRIT SAYS UNTO THE CHURCHES." (Revelation 2:7; 2:11; 2:17; 2:29; 3:6; 3:13; 3:22) There must be something extremely important within this statement the Lord wants us to recognize and understand. Not only did

He speak this phrase seven times, but He also linked "ears to hear" with being an overcomer in each case. The word "ear" in this passage speaks of **perceiving with the mind, understanding, and knowing**. The word "hear" in this passage means **to attend to, to consider, to perceive, to understand, and to comprehend**. Putting all this together, the Lord Jesus was painting a picture for us pertaining to the overcomers. In essence, an overcomer is one who perceives, knows, attends to, considers, understands, and comprehends the Word of God. The idea of understanding the Word of God will also spill over into our behavior, causing us to overcome sin, the flesh, and the carnal mind.

Most Christians spend a lifetime of *quoting* the Scriptures, but have very little *understanding* of what they are quoting. This is what I refer to as the "Pharisee Spirit". The Pharisees (along with the Sadducees and scribes) were the religious leaders of the day when Jesus walked the earth. They were constantly <u>trying</u> (though they never succeeded) to tempt and trap Jesus in His words in order to prove He was not the Messiah. They went about quoting Scriptures and making religious statements, but had absolutely no idea what any of it meant. THEY DID NOT "UNDERSTAND" ("HAVE EARS TO HEAR") WHAT THEY WERE SAYING. They were religious in their rhetoric, but their spiritual ears were deaf to the voice of the Son of God. This is why Jesus warned His disciples concerning "the doctrine of the Pharisees".

Matthew 16:5-12 states... "And when His disciples were come to the other side, they had forgotten to take bread. Then Jesus said unto them, Take heed and beware of **the leaven of the Pharisees and of the Sadducees**. And they reasoned among themselves, saying, It is because we have taken no bread. Which when Jesus perceived, He said unto them, O you of little faith, why reason you among yourselves, because you have brought no bread? Do you not yet **understand**, neither remember the five loaves of the five thousand, and how many baskets you took up? Neither the seven loaves of the four thousand, and how many baskets you took up? **How is it that you do not understand** that I spoke it not to you concerning bread, that you should **beware of the leaven of the Pharisees and of the Sadducees**? Then **understood** they how that He bade them not beware of the leaven of bread, but of **the doctrine of the Pharisees and of the Sadducees**."

Jesus also spoke of "HEARING" and "UNDERSTANDING" in the parable of the sower in Matthew 13:18-23. He told us of those who received seed by the way side, into stony places, among thorns, and <u>those who received seed into the good ground</u>. The theme of the entire parable is about "HEARING" and "UNDERSTANDING the word of the Kingdom". Those who received seed (the word of the Kingdom) into the good ground are those who "HEAR" the Word, and "UNDERSTAND" it. Once again, this is obviously talking about "ears to hear". Those with "ears to hear" will then go on to produce fruit in the Kingdom of God, and bring forth, some a hundredfold, some sixty, some thirty.

PAUL'S DESIRE FOR THE CHURCH AT EPHESUS

Paul's writings to the church at Ephesus are some of the most profound written words in the entire Bible. He takes us from the earthly realm into the heavenly realm where we find ourselves seated in heavenly places in Christ Jesus. Paul's desire for the church at Ephesus (and for the church in general) is clearly spelled out through the entire letter, but especially in two very climactic passages in chapters one and three.

In Ephesians 1:17-23 Paul prays that these believers in Christ would be given the "**spirit of wisdom and revelation in the knowledge of God: the eyes of their "UNDERSTANDING" being enlightened**; that they may **"KNOW"** what is the hope of God's calling, and what the riches of the glory of His inheritance in the saints..." He goes on to explain the exceeding greatness of God's power, in that He raised Christ from the dead, and that He also is raising up a body of believers (the body of Christ), in which ALL THE FULLNESS OF GOD SHALL BE MANIFESTED IN ALL THE EARTH! The words "spirit of wisdom and revelation in the knowledge of Him", "understanding", and "know" definitely speak of "ears to hear". Go back and read this passage again, meditating on what Paul was saying. He longed in his heart for those who called themselves believers to be given the "ears to hear" concerning the purpose and plan of God.

The other magnificent passage in the book of Ephesians which contains terminology similar to that of "ears to hear" is Ephesians 3:14-21. It states..."For this cause I bow my knees unto the Father of our Lord Jesus Christ, Of Whom the whole family in heaven and earth is named, That He would grant you, according to the riches of His glory, to be strengthened with might by His Spirit in the inner man; That Christ may dwell in your hearts by faith; that you, being rooted and grounded in love, **May be able to "comprehend"** with all saints what is the breadth, and length, and depth, and height; And to know the love of Christ, which passes knowledge, that you might be filled with all the fullness of God. Now unto Him that is able to do exceeding abundantly above all that we ask or think, according to the power that works in us, Unto Him be glory in the church by Christ Jesus throughout all ages (generations), world without end (unto the age of the ages). Amen.

Paul's desire for the church at Ephesus was no doubt his desire for all who named the name of Christ. It was this: He desired for those who were justified and had believed on the Lord Jesus Christ to be able to "COMPREHEND" ("HAVE EARS TO HEAR") the purpose and plan of God. Without this, my friend, we become nothing more than a bunch of religious "church-goers", pointing the finger at others who we think are not yet as good as we are. It is all about having "ears to hear" the purpose and plan of God. My good friend (and mentor) Dr. Harold Lovelace has written a book which all should read. It is entitled, "Read And Search God's **Plan**". Notice how he did not entitle it, "Read And Search God's Word", but rather, it is entitled, "Read And Search God's _**PLAN**_". Many people invest their entire life into studying God's Word, but never realize that HE HAS A PLAN! It takes "ears to hear" from the Spirit of the living God to even recognize that God has a plan, and then to understand what it is and how it will be carried out.

UNITY AND EARS TO HEAR

One of the most beautiful aspects of "ears to hear" is how it brings unity to an otherwise divided group of people. This is the only true way to establish unity in the body of Christ. If God's people are all plugged into the notion that we must have "ears to hear" what the Spirit is saying unto the churches, then we will automatically come in line with what God is doing and saying. The goal is not so much to be in unity with one another, as much as it is TO BE IN UNITY WITH THE SPIRIT OF GOD. If we are in unity with the Spirit of God, then we will naturally be in unity one with another. For example, my co-worker and good friend (who is also a mentor to me) Louis Thompson tells a story of how he and his son (Billy Thompson) differed in their beliefs concerning the Lord for some time, but they are now in one mind and one accord.

Louis felt impressed by the Lord to pray for "truth" and continued in this manner for approximately thirteen years. After having diligently prayed for "truth" for thirteen years, Louis came across a minister on the radio who began to give him the answer to his prayers. The Spirit of God spoke through this minister and his radio program, telling the listeners how they were to take a "position of testimony" while on the job, at the house, out in public, or wherever they were. This "position of testimony", which is our position IN CHRIST, made him free and set him on a journey in which he discovered all the things (truths) he had longed for in his time of diligent prayer before the Lord. Whenever Louis tells the story of how he received this knowledge, he will surely tell you how he rejoiced the day he heard it on the radio as he was driving on the interstate. It was so liberating to him that he actually pulled his car over onto the shoulder of the interstate, got out, and did a victory dance ("charismatic jig") as he celebrated before the Lord. The Lord had given Louis the Scriptural prescription which would bring knowledge, victory, and power. He no longer went to work, thinking that any one person or situation was his problem. He knew he did not have to try and fight with anyone or anything that came his way. He simply took his "position of testimony" and let the Lord fight his battles. He was in position to be used of the Lord and open and ready to "HEAR" from the Lord.

As Louis continued to listen to this particular radio program he gained even more knowledge of things he had read in the Bible all his life, but were now being QUICKENED to him to where he could see the true purpose and plan of God. He was especially drawn to 2nd Peter chapter one, which speaks of the **divine nature**. After coming to the revelation of what it meant to partake of God's divine nature, he was ushered into the most profound revelation he had ever received from the Lord. Louis began to come to the understanding that the Scriptures taught a reconciliation of all things (the ultimate salvation of all men) through the blood of the cross of Christ.

After Louis believed this for some time, it was brought to his attention (by his brother "Root Beer") that his son (Billy) believed in an ultimate salvation of all men through Jesus Christ. Louis told his brother he had already received this revelation and believed the same thing. Shortly after that Louis and his son got together to drink some coffee and talk things over. When they sat down at the table together and began to talk it was as if they had believed these things all their life and were on the same page concerning God ultimately saving all men. They were speaking the same language, using the same terminology, and in agreement, being in one mind and one accord. What could have possibly caused this to happen? Well…You guessed it…*__EARS TO HEAR__*! They had both tapped into "hearing what the Spirit is saying unto the churches". This makes all the difference in the world. They were the ones to first introduce me to this great truth. **I am so glad they did!**

HOW DO WE GET EARS TO HEAR?

One sure way to acquire "ears to hear" is to simply humble yourself and ask God to give you the ability to comprehend (by the Spirit) His Word. Whenever you become aware you are in need of something that you do not have it would be a good idea to just ask God to give it to you. I still believe the Scriptures when they say…"**Ask**, and it shall be given you; **seek**, and you shall find; **knock**, and it shall be opened unto you: For every one that asks receives; and he that seeks finds; and to him that knocks it shall be opened. Or what man is there of you, whom if his son ask bread, will he give him a stone? Or if he ask a fish, will he give him a serpent? If you then, being evil, know how to give good gifts unto your children, how much more shall your Father which is in heaven give good things to them that ask Him?" (Matthew 7:7-11) This is what we are called to do on our end. We are to simply recognize (as God reveals these things to us), submit, and partake of God's nature. He is actually the One doing the work in us. He awakens us to our need for "ears to hear" and then we humbly ask, seek, and knock for Him to do so.

Acquiring "ears to hear" is not an instantaneous thing, though. They are actually **developed** as we go through our sanctification process, in which God burns away our carnality, unclogging our spiritual ears in order for us to submit, partake, and manifest His life in the earth. The more we submit to His training, the more we develop a keen "ear to hear" Him, understanding and grasping the purpose and plan of God. We then become **stewards** of the mysteries of God, becoming **accountable** to the work God is doing in us. This is what **prepares** and **qualifies** us to be placed in a position of **rulership** in His Kingdom at the appointed time. Ask your Heavenly Father today to give you the "ears to hear" Him in all things. Hallelujah!

PART 12 - CHRIST IS "ALL", AND "IN ALL"

The information presented in this teaching was first brought to my attention by Dr. Harold Lovelace and his precious wife Louise. They have instilled in me the importance of being a Berean in search of Christ, the Son of the living God!

Colossians 3:10-11 is quite an astounding few verses of Scripture. I am afraid it is **little talked about and understood** by the casual reader of Scripture. It has within it one of the most precious revelations of the entire Bible. It is this: THE REVELATION OF CHRIST, THE SON OF GOD! Not only is this a revelation that is to be found within the Holy Scriptures, **but it is the fundamental revelation of all further revelation!** Now that I have your attention, let's take a look at these amazing verses of Scripture. They contain within them information which helps us to begin our journey in discovering THE UNSEARCHABLE RICHES OF CHRIST. Colossians 3:10-11 states…"And have put on the new man, which is renewed in knowledge after the image of Him that created him: Where there is neither Greek nor Jew, circumcision nor uncircumcision, **Barbarian, Scythian,** bond nor free: ___but Christ is all, and in all.___" What startling words! What did Paul mean by this? Who were the Barbarians and Scythians? What did he mean when he said that Christ is all, and in all. Why did he not say that Jesus is all, and in all? Is there a difference between Jesus and Christ? Let us dare to look into the unsearchable riches of Christ!

THE DIFFERENCE BETWEEN JESUS AND CHRIST

The first and most important point to see is that "Christ" was not the last name of Jesus. The word "Christ", which means *the anointed one - Messiah*, speaks of an office, description, or position. While it is common knowledge that Jesus was The Christ, The Son of the Living God, the understanding of Christ goes much deeper than just the One literal historical figure Who was named Jesus. The man Jesus represented humanity as a whole and fulfilled the office of the "Son of Man". This same man was also The Christ. In this sense He represented deity and fulfilled the office of the "Son of God". Hence, the Word (Which was God) was made flesh and dwelled among us. With this in mind, though, it is very interesting to note how the apostle Paul spoke of Christ in a plural sense, and even reaching back to the beginning of the ages. We will now point out some key passages of Scripture in order to better understand the Christ of God.

1st Corinthians 12:12 states…"For as **the body is one**, and **has many members**, and **all the members of that one body, being many**, are **one body: _SO ALSO IS CHRIST_**." *Notice how Paul refers to Christ as many members who all belong to one body*. Naturally, we do understand that the Lord Jesus is the Head of the body, but the truth that Christ is extended from the Head to the body is almost always overlooked and never mentioned. So…We must admit and come to terms with the corporate aspect of the Christ, Who is all, and in all.

Colossians 1:26-27 states…"Even the **mystery** which has been **hid from ages** and from generations, but **now is made manifest to His saints**: To whom God would make known what is the riches of the glory of this **mystery** among the Gentiles; which is **Christ in you**, the hope of glory…" *Notice how Paul refers to Christ as a mystery, and that the understanding of Christ has been hidden for ages. He then goes on to say how the mystery has been revealed to the saints. The revelation of the Christ is this: **Christ is in you**, the hope of glory*.

This next Scripture passage will further clarify what we have just stated concerning Christ being revealed in man throughout the ages. The verse I am referring to is 1st Corinthians 10:1-4. It states…"Moreover, brethren, I would not that you should be ignorant, how that all our fathers were under the cloud, and all passed through the sea; And were all baptized unto Moses in the cloud and in the sea; And did all eat the same **spiritual meat**; And did all drink the same **spiritual drink**: for **they drank of that spiritual Rock that followed them: and that Rock was Christ**." Well…This really begins to clear things up! *Notice how Paul refers to God's people eating and drinking of Christ about 1,500 years before Jesus was even born.* Are you beginning to get the picture? The word "Christ" is not just speaking of the historical Jesus Who walked the earth, but rather, it refers to the anointing and indwelling presence of God in man. Let's take a trip back to the book of Colossians to define Christ in even more specific terms.

Colossians 1:15 states…"(Christ) Who is the image of the invisible God, the firstborn of every creature…" This explanation pinpoints the purpose of Christ, putting it in very specific terms. It clearly states that CHRIST IS THE *IMAGE* OF THE INVISIBLE GOD! Can you now begin to see a clear picture and definition of the Christ of God? Did not God say in the beginning in Genesis 1:26…"Let Us make man in Our *IMAGE*, AFTER OUR LIKENESS…?" Well…There you have it! Christ is the image of the invisible God! The Christ of God speaks of man (the human race), in whom dwells the presence of the living God, who (man) is being made into the image of God. The Lord Jesus is of course the Head, and we are the body. He is The Christ (Anointed One), and we are His Christ (anointed ones), making up the body of Christ, THE IMAGE OF THE INVISIBLE GOD! Now that I have probably made some of you glad, and some of you mad, let's go even deeper into the unsearchable riches of Christ, looking into the magnificent statement made by Paul concerning Christ, Who is all, and in all, including the **Barbarians** and **Scythians**.

THE BARBARIANS AND SCYTHIANS

If the statement "Christ is all, and in all" is not startling enough to cause a person to dig into the understanding of Christ, then how about the statement that Paul made about the Barbarians and Scythians? Once again, the apostle Paul told us in Colossians 3:11…"There is neither Greek nor Jew, circumcision nor uncircumcision, **Barbarian**, **Scythian**, bond nor free…" Notice how Paul covers all areas of society, even down to those who are uncultured, such as the Barbarians and Scythians.

The word "Barbarian" means one whose speech is rude, rough, and harsh. It also speaks of one who speaks a foreign or strange language which is not understood by another. It was also used by the Greeks to mean any foreigner ignorant of the Greek language, whether mental or moral, with the added notion after the Persian War, of rudeness and brutality. The word "Scythian" also means rude or rough. **The Scythians, however, were regarded as the "wildest" of the Barbarians.** (Note: The **Scythians** flourished from the 8th to the 4th cent. BC. They spoke an Indo-Iranian language _**but had no system of writing**_.) Was Paul actually saying that Christ was all, and in all men, including the uncultured and those of the lowest level of society such as the Barbarians and Scythians? Is it true that the Kingdom of God is in every man (including the Pharisees who Jesus spoke to in Luke 17:20-21) waiting to be discovered, but it is not seen (perceived) until the person is born again? Oh the wonder of it all!!! In order to answer these questions we will now lean on the words of two great men of God (Dr. Harold Lovelace & J. Preston Eby) who will dare to take on this subject and answer these all-important questions.

According to Dr. Harold Lovelace:

"A thought for today comes from Colossians chapter three. Read the entire chapter paying close attention to every word. Now go back over all the phrases and see all the instructions. Next…In verse eleven are listed eight groups, which CHRIST IS ALL, AND IN ALL. Next…Now pay close attention to ONE group -"Scythian"- and remember that Christ is all, and in all. Paul has already given a broad list that Christ is in, but I want you to pay close attention to this one particular group.

In Phillips Bible: savage. In Taylor Bible: In this new life one's nationality or race or education or social position is unimportant. Such things mean nothing.

In Peloubet's Bible Dictionary: Scythian as a generalized term for rude, ignorant, degraded. The name often included all the nomadic tribes, who dwelt mostly on the north of the Black and the Caspian Sea, stretching thence indefinitely into inner Asia and **were regarded by the ancients as standing extremely low in point of intelligence and civilization.**

Webster's New World Dictionary: Scyth-i-a (sith'e-a) ancient region in SE Europe, centered about the N coast of the Black Sea. Syth-i-a of ancient Scythia, its people, their language, etc. 1. any of a nomadic tribe and warlike people who lived in ancient Scythia. 2. their extinct Iranian language.

Think about this...Paul wrote that...Christ is in the Greeks (wisdom) and Jews (religion), even down to this broad category of people who are uncultured. He even spoke of those in jail or out. In all of this broad range of humanity Christ is in ALL PEOPLE to the lowest level of society. It then goes on to tell us in verse 16..."Let the word of Christ dwell in you 'richly' in all wisdom..."

Lord help us all to INCLUDE ALL as you have! May we make this clear to ALL...explicitly CLEAR!" -end quote- (Dr. Harold Lovelace)

According to J. Preston Eby:

"You remember that when the Pharisees asked Jesus when the Kingdom of God should come, He answered, "The kingdom of God comes not with observation...for lo, the kingdom of God *is within you.*" The Pharisees were treating as future what was already present. The Kingdom of God was right there *within them* if they could have understood it. "But," someone objects, "surely the Kingdom of God was not within those carnal, hateful, legalistic, Christ-rejecting Pharisees!" Some say that the correct translation should be:

For the kingdom of God is "*in your midst,*" or "*among you,*" meaning that the Kingdom was present in their midst in the person of Jesus, "among" them but not "within" them. It cannot be denied—the Kingdom was indeed present among them in the very life of the Son of God, the King of glory! **But that is not the meaning of this passage.**

The clearest meaning of the Greek can always be ascertained by *usage*. The way a word is *used* reveals its true meaning—the meaning that the Holy Spirit of inspiration puts upon it, not the meaning our English translators give it. It is a thing of wonder—the Holy Spirit has faithfully, powerfully, wisely and indisputably recorded for us the precise meaning of the word here translated "within". The Greek word is "ENTOS" meaning simply, according to Strong's Concordance, "inside; within". The word is used in only one other place in the New Testament, in Matthew 23:26. It is the Lord Jesus Himself that uses the word on both occasions, and notice what He says. "Woe unto you, scribes and Pharisees, hypocrites! for you make clean the *outside* of the cup and platter, but *within* they are full of extortion and excess. You blind Pharisee, cleanse first that which is *within* ("entos") the cup and platter, that the *outside* of them may be clean also." No one can argue that "ENTOS" means "in the midst" or "among" in this place—it clearly means "within". "Within" is contrasted with the "outside" of the cup and platter and plainly speaks of the pollution *within* the hearts of men, not *in their midst* or *among* them. The evil in men is not something apart from them or outside of them but something rooted deeply in the inward nature.

The question follows—how could Jesus say to the same Pharisees that both corruption was within them and the Kingdom of God was within them? It sounds like an obvious contradiction. But it isn't. Paul spoke of a dual reality within man when he said, "For I delight in the law of God after the *inward man:* but I see another **law *in my members,*** warring against the law of my (spiritual) mind, and bringing me into captivity to the law of sin which is in my members" (Rom. 7:22-23). Little wonder that in desperation he cried out, "O wretched man that I am!" It is really very simple. The carnal, soulish heart of man is the seat of all uncleanness, just as the deeper spirit of man is the root of all godliness. So it is not surprising that the Pharisees failed to discover the presence of the Kingdom within them, for they were not walking after the Spirit, but after the flesh. Yet they were potentially capable of either." -end quote- (The Kingdom Of God, J. Preston Eby)

ACCESSING THE CHRIST & THE KINGDOM OF GOD
THAT IS WITHIN

Please do not misunderstand what is being said here in this teaching. This teaching is not meant to say that all men are already saved without having to go through the blood of the cross of Christ, and that there is no need for repentance and the born again experience. What is being stated, though, is that God has placed the dual reality of the spirit and soul in every man. Man lives out of his soulish realm until the day he is born again, in which he can then see (perceive) the Kingdom of God (Christ in us, the hope of glory) which is within ("entos"). The Christ (presence and anointing of God), which is all, and in all, is buried under a mountain of wood, hay, and stubble (carnality) until the time we begin to call on the name of the Lord. At this time (the time of our justification and Passover experience in the Lord), we are made aware that it is Christ in us the hope of glory, AND THE CHRIST LIFE IS MADE MANIFEST TO US! Remember…"Christ is a mystery which has been hidden for ages, BUT NOW IS MADE MANIFEST TO GOD'S SAINTS…" (Colossians 1:26)

So…The saints of God who have been born again (born from above or awakened by the Spirit of God) are the ones to whom the Christ has been revealed to. They now know it is in them, the hope of glory. It takes an experience with our Heavenly Father to have this revealed to us. Do you remember what was said in Matthew 16:15-17? It states…"He (Jesus) said unto them, But whom say you that I am? And Simon Peter answered and said, You are **the Christ, the Son** of the living God. And Jesus answered and said unto him, Blessed are you, Simon Barjona: **for flesh and blood has not _"revealed"_ it unto you, but My Father which is in heaven."**

Receiving revelation from the Father concerning the Christ in us, the hope of glory, opens the door which leads us to **partake** of the new man. We are to actually put on the new man, for Paul said in Colossians 3:9-10…"Lie not one to another, seeing that **you have put off the old man with his deeds; And have put on the new man**, which is renewed in knowledge **after the image of Him** that created him…" Once again, we are able to see the dual reality which exists in man. Paul describes it here as the old man and the new man. It could also be looked at in several other ways, such as: the tree of the knowledge of good and evil versus the tree of life, the carnal mind versus the mind of Christ, the soul versus the spirit of man, and the spirit of antichrist versus the spirit of Christ.

Once we are born again to see (perceive) the Kingdom of God (righteousness, peace, and joy in the Holy Ghost) that operates from within, we are then ushered into a lifestyle of putting on or partaking of what we have been awakened to and given through the death, burial, and resurrection of the Lord Jesus Christ. The apostle Peter also spoke of this (2nd Peter chapter 1) in terms of **partaking of the divine nature.** Christ in us, the hope of glory, could also be looked at as the character and nature of God, for remember…Christ is the image of the invisible God. Every man (every man in his own order - 1st Corinthians 15:23) shall come forth in the image of the invisible God in the fullness of time. The purpose of this age is to gather in a remnant, followed by the nations in the coming age, ending with every knee bowing and every tongue confessing Jesus Christ as Lord in the age of the ages. Make no mistake about it…Christ is all, and in all, for our God is all in all (1st Corinthians 15:28)!

PART 13 - MY THOUGHTS ARE NOT YOUR THOUGHTS

How many times have you heard someone say…"God's thoughts are not our thoughts, and God's ways are not our ways?" While this is a legitimate Scripture that should be quoted, most people use it to support foolish traditions or the doctrines of men. For example, it has come to my attention that this Scripture is a favorite among those who belong to the eternal torture camp. They usually quote it to justify their ridiculous teaching, which states that God will take the vast majority of the human race and separate, vindictively punish, and torture them forever. When they are asked to account for the asininity of this teaching, knowing it does not make sense or paint a loving and powerful picture of their Savior, they usually pull out their trump card, quoting Isaiah 55:8-9, which states…"For My thoughts are not your thoughts, neither are your ways My ways, says the LORD. For as the heavens are higher than the earth, so are My ways higher than your ways, and My thoughts than your thoughts." They even say things like…"God's plan is not supposed to make sense to us," using these verses to support such a ludicrous statement. Once again, this is another classic case where a Scripture is quoted by many, but little understood and checked into. If Christians would simply take the time to read before and after the verse they are quoting, then they would be educated as to what they are talking about, grasping the spirit and meaning of what they quote, not just repeating words with little or no understanding of what they are talking about. Since this verse is quoted so often to support many different things, let's take a look at what is actually being said in order to rightly divide this passage.

MERCY

Let's start by taking a fresh look at this passage of Scripture, including the verse right before it. Isaiah 55:7-9 states…"Let the wicked forsake his way, and the unrighteous man his thoughts: and let him return unto the LORD, and **He will have mercy** upon him; and to our God, for **He will abundantly pardon**. For My thoughts are not your thoughts, neither are your ways My ways, says the LORD. For as the heavens are higher than the earth, so are My ways higher than your ways, and My thoughts than your thoughts." After taking a look at these verses in context we are able to see that the subject matter is THE MERCY OF GOD. This is what we are to understand when we declare that God's thoughts are not our thoughts, and His ways are not our ways. Yes…God is going to judge and correct the wicked ways of men, causing them to return to Him, but we must see that His MERCY is far greater than we have ever imagined. God will have mercy on all and abundantly pardon when we are brought to the place of repentance by His dealings with us.

It is also important to point out at this time that ALL of God's dealings with man are of the ages (within the ages / age-lasting), for the purpose of correction, and end in mercy! As I write of God's great mercy, I am reminded of four passages of Scripture which testify to this very thing. They are Romans 11:32, Ephesians 2:4, James 2:13, and James 5:11. There are many Scriptures which speak of God's mercy, but these four in particular are extremely helpful, causing us to see the true nature and character of our Heavenly Father, which is LOVE, in that He will have mercy on all. It will be our goal to quote and comment on each verse, painting a clear picture of our God Who will abundantly pardon and have mercy on all.

ROMANS 11:32

Romans 11:32 states…"For God has concluded them all in unbelief, that He might have mercy upon all." Here is the same verse from Today's English version, which states…"For God has made all people prisoners of disobedience, so that He might show mercy to them all." This verse tells us that not only is God going to have mercy, BUT HE IS GOING TO HAVE MERCY ON ALL PEOPLE! Hallelujah…This sure sounds like **Good News** to me! The word "mercy" in this verse means *kindness or good will towards the miserable and the afflicted, joined with a desire to help them.* With this in mind, it makes perfect sense for God to have mercy on all, for HE IS THE ONE Who has subjected us to vanity, afflicted us that we might learn His statutes, and locked all of us in disobedience in order that He might reveal His mercy to us. In case you have a hard time believing this, Romans 11:36 tells us…"For of Him, and through Him, and to Him, are all things: to Whom be glory forever. Amen." This clearly tells us that all things came out from God, are sustained through Him, and will return to Him. In fact, this **proves** that God will have mercy on all; for it states that **all things are to Him** (all things will be reconciled and return to Him in the fullness of time). To help make this point, we will now turn our attention to a quote from Dr. Stephen Jones.

According to Dr. Stephen Jones:

"When God called Abraham and chose him and his descendants for a special purpose in the earth, the rest of the world remained in darkness and blindness. It was not that God wanted to keep them in darkness for ever, else God would be unjust. Rather, God made Israel the peculiar treasure that would be His excuse for buying the whole field (world).

Hence, He blinded Israel in order that He might bring judgment upon her and cast her out of His house. The seed of Israel was thus sown in the field to bring an abundant harvest to God. Meanwhile, God also purchased the field, lest He harvest in another man's field, or steal treasure hidden in another man's field. So the world was blessed through Israel's blindness and *"obtained mercy through their unbelief."* Paul's final conclusion of the matter is found in verse 32:

> **32 For God has concluded** [sugkleio, "locked up, or shut up"] **them all in unbelief, that He might have mercy upon all.**

Good News: Mercy Upon All

Paul then breaks out into praise for His majesty, power, and goodness for His great plan for creation.

> **33 O the depth of the riches both of the wisdom and knowledge of God! How unsearchable are His judgments, and His ways past finding out!**

> **34 For who has known the mind of the Lord? Or who has been His counselor?**

> **35 Or who has first given to Him, and it shall be recompensed unto him again?**

> **36 For of Him, and through Him, and to** [into] **Him, are all things; to Whom be glory for ever. Amen.**

Paul is anything but a doom-and-gloom preacher. He revels in the judgments of God. He stands in awe of His ways. He does not presume to be God's counselor by telling Him what He ought to do, but shouts AMEN to all that God is doing. Paul has begun to understand the ways of God, and so he does not hesitate to agree fully with the plan of God in locking both Israel and the world in blindness for a season. Why? Because *out of* Him, and *through* Him, and *into* Him are all things.

These words indicate that all things ORIGINATE in God; all things are processed THROUGH Him, and all things are going back INTO Him. This is just another way of saying that in the end, God will be all in all (1 Cor. 15:28). He will not be All in just a few, nor in a tiny remnant, nor will He be limited to all Israel. He will be all IN ALL." -end quote- (<u>Blindness In Part</u>, Dr. Stephen Jones)

EPHESIANS 2:4-7

Ephesians 2:4-7 states…"But **God, Who is rich in mercy, for His great love** wherewith He loved us, Even when we were dead in sins, has quickened us together with Christ, (by grace you are saved;) And has raised us up together, and made us sit together in heavenly places in Christ Jesus: That in the ages to come **He might show the exceeding riches of His grace in His kindness toward us through Christ Jesus.**" If you were wondering whether or not your Heavenly Father is merciful, this passage does a pretty good job of clearing up the matter. Not only is our Father merciful, BUT HE IS RICH IN MERCY! He begins by shedding His grace and mercy on a remnant of people, who will then be used to be an extension of this same mercy, showing forth THE **EXCEEDING RICHES** OF HIS GRACE IN HIS KINDNESS to others in the **ages to come**. Well…Now we can see that not only is God **rich in mercy**, but **He is EXCEEDINGLY RICH in mercy and grace**. He is so full of mercy that He needs **ages and ages** to demonstrate even a small measure of His great mercy. At this present time He has quickened and raised (justified) a firstfruits company. His mercy, which is now at work in this firstfruits company of believers, is going to grow and grow until the earth is filled with the knowledge of the glory of the Lord, as the waters cover the sea (Isaiah 11:9 & Habakkuk 2:14).

Hebrews 8:11-12 also speaks of the earth being filled with the knowledge of God in the ages to come, and that God will be merciful to all. It states… "And they shall not teach every man his neighbor, and every man his brother, saying, Know the Lord: for **all shall know Me,** from the least to the greatest. **For I will be <u>"MERCIFUL"</u> to their unrighteousness,** and their sins and their iniquities will I remember no more."

Are you getting the picture yet? God's purpose of the ages will end in mercy for all. He has purposely designed it this way, setting it (His purpose) up by locking (shutting) everyone up in disobedience in order that He might have mercy on all men. When we begin to understand the purpose of the law, we will see that it has always been God's intention to show mercy to all, for this is the very purpose of the law. Many think of God's law as obsolete due to the fact we are now under grace, but God forbid that we should do away with His law, for it is His character and nature. Remember…Jesus did not come to destroy the law, but to fulfill it (Matthew 5:17)! In actuality, the law of God has two main purposes, which are: 1. To convict of sin, being a schoolmaster which leads us to the grace of God through Christ, in which we become partakers of the divine nature…&…2. To bring about the mercy of our Heavenly Father. Some of you are probably wondering how the law could possibly bring about the mercy of God. Well…Let's take a look.

JAMES 2:13 / MERCY TRIUMPHS OVER JUDGMENT / THE MERCY FACTOR

Very few Christians understand the purpose of God's law. In fact, it (the law) has become an element of mass confusion among believers. If we do not take the time to understand the types and shadows of the Old Testament, including the feasts of the Lord, the law, the prophets, and the Psalms, then we will be **very limited** in our understanding of the purpose and plan of God. As a matter of fact, this is exactly what Jesus told us to do. In Luke 24:44-45, we find Jesus talking to His disciples after His resurrection. He urges them to consider what was "written in **the Law of Moses**, and in **the Prophets**, and in **the Psalms** concerning Him." Here is what it states…"And He (Jesus) said unto them, These are the words which I spoke unto you, while I was yet with you, that all things must be fulfilled, which were written in **the Law of Moses**, and in **the Prophets**, and in **the Psalms**, concerning Me. **Then opened He their <u>understanding</u>, that they might <u>understand</u> the scriptures…**"

As we take the time to go back to the law, the prophets, and the Psalms, we will see beyond a shadow of a doubt that they do indeed paint a beautiful picture of the Lord Jesus Christ, God's purpose of the ages, and that God's desire is to have all men made in His image, being corrected, refined, and restored by His great mercy. Here are a few things to consider concerning God's law, and how it contains within it the "mercy factor", which will ultimately cause God to have mercy on all men…

According to Dr. Stephen Jones:

"We have not fully appreciated the statement in James 2:13, "mercy rejoices against judgment" (KJV), or "mercy triumphs over judgment" (NASB). Let me explain.

James, the brother of Jesus, was the first leader ("bishop") of the Church in Jerusalem. James was well versed in the Scriptures (i.e., the Old Testament). No doubt he had studied the Ark of the Covenant and had seen how its construction manifested the mind of God insofar as the law's application and administration.

The Ark itself was a box made of wood overlaid with gold (Ex. 25:10, 11). Wood speaks of humanity or human flesh, while gold speaks of the divine nature. This combination of wood overlaid with gold prophesied of the ultimate purpose for man's creation, which is to take human flesh, made of the dust of the ground, and overlay it with gold in order to manifest the glory of God in human flesh.

Within the Ark were three things: the two tablets of the law (Deut. 10:5), Aaron's rod (Num. 17:10), and an omer of manna (Ex. 16:33). See also Heb. 9:4, where they are listed together.

These signified *the law, the authority* to administer it, and *the Word* of God (and Christ Who is the Word made flesh).

When Heb. 8:10 speaks of God writing the law in our hearts by the New Covenant, this is pictured as the Ark housing the tablets of the law. Those who have the law written in their hearts are those who have ears to hear what the Spirit is saying to the Church (the manna). These are also the administrators of the law, on behalf of the rest of humanity, until such time as all come to the knowledge of God for themselves. This is the purpose of the New Covenant (Heb. 8:11).

As bishop of Jerusalem, James certainly would have studied this carefully in order to know how to administer the law with justice and mercy in the Church. He took note that the mercy seat was positioned on top of the Ark itself and was made of pure gold (Ex. 25:17). We read in Exodus 25:21,

"And you shall <u>put the mercy seat on top of the ark</u>, and in the ark you shall put the testimony which I shall give you."

Hence, James says, *"mercy triumphs over judgment."* The translators may not have understood that James' statement was referencing the Ark of the Covenant, or they probably would have translated it: "<u>mercy exults (or is exalted in position) over justice</u>."

The law, of course, administers divine justice. The Greek word used by James is *krisis*, which (according to Strong's Concordance) means "decision (for or against); a tribunal; by implication justice (specifically, divine law)." In other words, it has to do with making a decision in regard to two disagreeing parties about what is right and what is wrong. Many think that *judgment* is a purely negative word, and no one wants to be "under judgment," because they think it is synonymous with *condemnation*. But in reality, judgment is neutral, because in a dispute both sides are judged, but only one side is right and is certainly not condemned (ruled against).

A better word to use, then, which conveys a more accurate picture in today's world, is *justice*. True justice is determined by the divine law. Man's laws are often unjust in themselves, and when this problem is combined with the problem of having imperfect administrators of the law (judges), there can be much injustice in a nation, as most people are aware. But divine justice is perfect, by Biblical definition, for it reflects the mind of God.

The only real problem arose when God appointed men as administrators of the law in the lower courts on earth. The administration of the law has often become hardened and legalistic in its application. This is a particular problem among those who have not studied the Ark of the Covenant itself and therefore do not understand that *"mercy exults over justice."*

In that same sense, the mercy seat COVERS the Ark of the Covenant. It is positioned above the tables of the law. The term also means "to exult, to exalt, to triumph, and to rejoice." James uses the term as a perfect play on words. Even as the mercy seat is exalted over the law, so also does mercy triumph in the end, and, in fact, mercy rejoices even as the winner of a contest rejoices in winning the prize.

Even as God makes a distinction between the Ark and the mercy seat, so also is there a distinction between the law and its administration. One can have the law and still administer it incorrectly (or without mercy), and this often happened in the history of Israel.

It is only when the King administers the law with mercy that true righteousness is established in the land. This is the mind of Christ, before Whose tribunal all shall stand (Rom. 14:10).

Jesus never put away the law when He was called to administer it. He was certainly accused of it by those legalists who did not understand the mercy factor. But even in the case of the woman caught in adultery (John 8:3-11), He did not put away the law, but rendered judgment according to the law of jealousy found in Numbers 5, as I have shown earlier. In the Sabbath issues that topped the list of accusations, Jesus showed that God was more interested in mercy than in rigid, man-made rules defining "rest." -end quote- (Mercy Triumphs Over Justice, Dr. Stephen Jones)

Once again, we are able to see that mercy is at the very heart of our loving Heavenly Father. How is it that so many of God's good people are not able to see His mercy as triumphing over His judgment? Yes...God hates sin, lawlessness, and wickedness, but He surely does not hate the sinner! He has built the **"mercy factor"** into His own law in order that **all of His judgment, wrath, punishment, and vengeance shall end in CORRECTION, RESTORATION, AND MERCY!** <u>HE IS NOT THE ETERNAL TORTURER</u> THAT MOST OF CHRISTIANITY HAS MADE HIM OUT TO BE! HE IS THE ALL-POWERFUL, ALL-LOVING, AND ALL-MERCIFUL SAVIOR OF THE WORLD!

There is one more Scripture we are going to consider as we crescendo and build up to the grand finale of mercy Scriptures. This Scripture (James 5:11) leaves us with no doubt concerning the character and nature of our Father, which is one of forgiveness, love, compassion, and mercy. There is much to be gained from a verse such as this, for it tells us of the "end of the Lord" as far as His dealings with man are concerned, and that they end in mercy.

JAMES 5:11

James 5:11 is a key Scripture along with the others we have mentioned concerning the mercy of God. It tells us of *God's main objective or goal* as far as how He deals with those in the human race. It states..."Behold, we count them happy which endure. You have heard of the patience of Job, and have seen the end of the Lord; that the Lord is very pitiful, and of tender mercy." This phrase (the Lord is very pitiful, and of tender mercy) means that **the end goal of God is to be full of pity and extremely compassionate**. Well...This settles it! No matter how stern our Father must be and will be at times to correct us, He will ultimately have mercy on the souls of men, reconciling all things unto Himself. It is His goal to have mercy on all. Despite what is taught by most in the realm of Evangelical Christianity, it is not the goal of God to eternally torture anyone. He desires to show us the exceeding riches of His grace and mercy. Remember... Isaiah 55:7-9 states..."Let the wicked forsake his way, and the unrighteous man his thoughts: and let him return unto the LORD, and **He will have mercy** upon him; and to our God, for **He will abundantly pardon**. For My thoughts are not your thoughts, neither are your ways My ways, says the LORD. For as the heavens are higher than the earth, so are My ways higher than your ways, and My thoughts than your thoughts."

We are now able to see the thoughts and ways of God. They are MERCY, PARDON, AND FORGIVENESS. Surely you can now see how God's thoughts and ways are not our thoughts and ways, and that His thoughts and ways are higher than ours. Man's way is to be unmerciful, condemning, and unforgiving. Surely you can see how man's thoughts and ways are lower than the ways of God. We must stop trying to pull God down to the level of the pathetic ways of man. Our Heavenly Father is not bent toward revenge, vindictiveness, and eternal torture that serves no redemptive purpose. Those are the lower ways of carnal man which are despicable in the eyes of God.

How fitting it is to close with the beautiful words of Gary Amirault, which state…

Punish He will, for our Father is just
In age-long correction, you surely can trust.
On vindictive torment our Father's not bent
Mercy will, *yes!* triumph over judgment.

PART 14 - QUALIFIED FOR THE PRIZE

The apostle Paul makes a **very interesting** statement in 1st Corinthians 9:24-27. It is of the utmost importance that we seek to understand what this statement means, for it contains within it key information which describes the sanctification process of the believer, including information about *qualifying* for the **prize** of the high calling of God in Christ Jesus. Here is the verse as it reads from the New International Version..."Do you not know that in a race all the runners run, but only one gets the **prize**? Run in such a way as to get the **prize**. Everyone who competes in the games goes into strict training. They do it to get a **crown** that will not last; but we do it to get a **crown** that will last forever. Therefore I do not run like a man running aimlessly; I do not fight like a man beating the air. No, I beat my body and make it my slave **so that after I have preached to others, I myself will not be disqualified for the prize.**"

Note: The NIV Bible translates ADOKIMOS as "disqualified for the prize." NIV Study Bible notes here reference 1st Corinthians 3 related to receiving rewards, and hence imply or interpret Paul in 9:27 as fearing a loss of rewards (and that may be why NIV has an "expanded" translation for ADOKIMOS of "disqualified for the prize", rather than simply "disqualified.").

One other Scripture with similar terminology which will shed light on the subject at hand is Philippians 3:10-14. It states..."That I may know Him, and **the power of His resurrection,** and the fellowship of His sufferings, being made conformable unto His death; **If by any means I might attain unto the resurrection of the dead. Not as though I had already attained, either were already perfect**: but I follow after, if that I may apprehend that for which also I am apprehended of Christ Jesus. Brethren, **I count not myself to have apprehended**: but this one thing I do, forgetting those things which are behind, and reaching forth unto those things which are before, **I press toward the mark for the prize of the high calling of God in Christ Jesus.**"

What was Paul talking about in these two passages of Scripture? Surely he must have been referring to something other than his salvation (justification) experience with the Lord Jesus Christ. He knew that was secure, and that nothing could separate him from the love of God in Christ Jesus. It must have been something more specific that Paul longed to be a part of when he referred to *the prize of the high calling of God in Christ Jesus*. It was something so wonderful that Paul wanted to make sure he would not be disqualified.

THE PRIZE / THE CROWN / THE 1ST RESURRECTION / KINGS AND PRIESTS / REIGN WITH HIM

The word "qualify" means: to make competent or eligible for an office, position, or task. With this in mind, we are now able to see what Paul was referring to. Paul knew there were going to be those who would be used by God in the ages to come, being put in positions of leadership in order to rule and reign for the purpose of gathering all nations, all people, and all things unto God through the blood of the cross of Christ. He also knew that God would not put people in these positions unless they had been qualified, tested, sanctified, and proven. Surely this makes sense, for we see this at work in the earth realm now, every day, and in all situations.

When a person goes for a job interview, what is it that the hiring party wants to know? Well…You guessed it. They want to know if the person they are interviewing is qualified to fill the position they are hiring for. What does a country (those in a democracy) look for when determining who is to be their president? What does a coach (in any sport) look for when determining who will be on the 1st team (those who fill the starting positions) of his roster? Those who are in charge in all of the scenarios that were just presented are looking for one thing: IS THE PERSON QUALIFIED TO FILL THE OFFICE, POSITION, OR TASK? Why should we think it a strange thing then that God wants His leaders to be qualified before placing them in a position of leadership? The fact that we look for qualification in this earthly realm before placing someone in a certain position tells us this idea first originated with God. This is where we learned it from. Our Heavenly Father knows better than to put a person in an office in which they are not qualified to handle. As we look into the words "prize", "crown", "the first resurrection", "kings and priests", and "reign with Him", we will understand what Paul was talking about and what he wanted to be a part of. These terms (though different) all point us in the right direction concerning what we are being qualified for.

The Prize:

The word "prize" (as used in 1st Corinthians 9:24 and Philippians 3:14) speaks of *the award given to the victor in a contest or game, a prize.* This is obviously a metaphor to describe those who will receive **rewards** from the Lord for having put on the character and nature of their Heavenly Father through having submitted to the process of being a partaker of God's divine nature. In other words (like Paul said), run in such a way as to get the prize. If you are going to serve the Lord, then serve Him all the way! Lay it all on the line as though you were running in a race to receive a prize (reward). If there is a prize at stake for those who serve the Lord, submitting to His purpose and plan, would you not want to receive it? God wants you to receive it. So…Run this Christian race with faith as though you want to be a part of those who are pressing toward the ultimate prize of the high calling of God in Christ Jesus. It is ultimately God's business who He gives rewards to and who He does not, but once again, run as though you are pressing toward the mark for the prize of the high calling of God in Christ Jesus. Does a runner who runs in a race run as though he believes he will not get the prize? If he is serious about the race, then he enters the race believing he can win. Why should we not run with faith as though we believe God is a big enough God to cause us to run to win the prize which is at stake?

The Crown:

The word "crown" (as used in 1st Corinthians 9:25) means: a mark of royal or (in general) exalted rank, including the wreath or garland which was given as a prize to victors in public games. It is interesting to note how Paul referred to this "crown" as an **incorruptible crown**. The word "incorruptible" refers to something which is *uncorrupted, not liable to corruption or decay, imperishable*. It is the same language Paul used in 1st Corinthians 15:42-54 to describe the condition of immortality (as it pertains to the body) given to the risen dead. With this in mind, it is quite obvious that the word "crown" refers to the glorified and resurrected body which shall be given to those who are qualified and placed in a position of royalty, serving as kings under the King of kings. As I write about this precious "crown", I am reminded of the words to one of my favorite songs. They are:

Little is much when God is in it!
Labor not for wealth or fame.
There's a <u>crown</u>—and you can win it,
If you go in Jesus' Name.

After covering a subject such as the incorruptible crown of the Lord (which speaks of that incorruptible body the overcomers are to receive at the appointed time), we are naturally led to what all of this speaks of, which is: THE FIRST RESURRECTION. To understand the first resurrection, is to understand the very heart of what Paul was referring to when he mentioned how he longed to qualify for the *prize (or crown)* of the high calling of God in Christ Jesus. The understanding of this is clearly spelled out in Philippians 3:10-14, Hebrews 11:35, and Revelation 20:4-6.

The First Resurrection:

We have already covered the topic of resurrection in an earlier teaching in this book, but it will be helpful and useful to go over a few key things again at this time in order to explain the subject at hand. We will start by going over some of the words and phrases used by Paul in Philippians 3:10-14. By putting all of this together, we will be able to get a clear picture of what Paul was pressing into, and just exactly what he meant when he spoke of the *prize of the high calling of God in Christ Jesus.*

According to Dr. Stephen Jones:

"When God told Moses to build TWO trumpets in Numbers 10:2, He distinguished between the rulers and the congregation (Church). When Jesus, Paul, and John spoke of two resurrections in the New Testament, they added to the prophecy, showing that the rulers will be raised in the first resurrection, and the Church will be raised later in the second.

The apostle Paul continues this distinction in Philippians 3:10, 11, saying,

"That I may know Him [Christ], and the power of His resurrection and the fellowship of His sufferings, being conformed to His death; in order that I may attain to the resurrection from the dead [Greek: exanastasis ek nekron]."

Dr. Bullinger comments on this passage in his marginal notes in The Companion Bible. He tells us that the Greek word "exanastasis ek nekron" means OUT-RESURRECTION FROM AMONG THE DEAD. He says that the normal term used is simply "anastasis nekron," which is the resurrection of the dead--meaning all of the dead. But "EXanastasis EK nekron," he says, "implies the resurrection of some, the former of these two classes, the others behind left behind."

In other words, Paul was telling the Philippian Church that his desire was to attain the FIRST resurrection--the limited resurrection out from among the rest of the dead. Paul had no doubt that he would be resurrected. But he knew of a "better resurrection" (Heb. 11:35) that would occur 1,000 years before the general resurrection (Rev. 20:5). Paul did not doubt his salvation, but he did express concern that he might not attain this resurrection out from among the dead. Thus he continues in Phil. 3:12, saying,

"NOT THAT I HAVE ALREADY OBTAINED IT, or have already become perfect, but I press on in order that I may lay hold of that for which also I was laid hold of by Christ Jesus."

What is "it" that he had not yet obtained? He had certainly already qualified for the general resurrection as a citizen of the Kingdom. But he knew that "enduring to the end" was required to inherit the first resurrection and to rule with Christ during the thousand years of the Tabernacles Age.

So we see that understanding Moses' two trumpets opens up a whole new realm of prophetic understanding. It makes us more aware of the difference between a Passover Christian and a Tabernacles ruler ("the sons of God")." -end quote- (<u>Moses' Two Trumpets In Prophecy</u>, Dr. Stephen Jones)

Now we are able to see beyond a shadow of a doubt what Paul was pressing toward, and what he meant by the *prize of the high calling of God in Christ Jesus*. He was referring to the **FIRST RESURRECTION**. He even mentions the fact that the "Lord Jesus Christ shall change our vile body, that it may be fashioned like unto His glorious body" in the last verse (verse 21) of the passage. This is obviously the heart of what he is talking about, for he concludes the passage by referring to God having the ability to give us a glorified, incorruptible, immortal, and resurrected body.

Hebrews 11:35 is another Scripture that distinguishes between the first and second resurrection, telling us there is **a prize to be obtained** by those who submit to the dealings of God for the purpose of being qualified for leadership. It states…"Women received their dead raised to life again: and others were tortured, not accepting deliverance; **that they might obtain a better resurrection**…" This piece of information (concerning a **better** resurrection) sheds a tremendous amount of light on the prize which is at stake for the overcomer in God's Kingdom. It clearly tells us of a BETTER resurrection. This would naturally lead us to believe there is another resurrection which will not contain within it the benefits of this better resurrection (the first resurrection) which is here mentioned by Paul in The Hall of Faith Chapter (Hebrews chapter 11). This statement helps us to further clarify and define the reward (prize) which awaits those who submit to the training of the Lord. Once again, that which awaits those who press toward the mark for the prize of the high calling of God in Christ Jesus - that which we are being qualified for - is a **better** resurrection. As we just stated, Paul refers to it as a "better resurrection", but John (in his writings in the book of Revelation) refers to it as the "first resurrection". John's comments on the first resurrection give us specific details as to who will be a part of this event, including an explanation of the purpose for this first resurrection.

Revelation 20:4-6 states… "And I saw **thrones**, and they sat upon them, and **judgment** was given unto them: and I saw the souls of them that were **beheaded** for the witness of Jesus, and for the Word of God, and which had **not worshipped the beast, neither his image, neither had received his mark** upon their foreheads, or in their hands; and **they lived and reigned with Christ a thousand years. But the rest of the dead lived not again until the thousand years were finished. This is the first resurrection. Blessed and holy is he that has part in the first resurrection**: on such the second death has no power, but **they shall be priests** of God and of Christ, **and shall reign with him a thousand years.**"

Not only does this passage tell us there will be a first resurrection, but it tells us who will be a part of this climactic event. It even explains what we are to expect from those who participate in this honor, describing how they will operate and manifest the Son of God to all those on the earth. We are told there will be people who sit on thrones. This speaks in a spiritual sense of the office of a king, telling us they will be given AUTHORITY, and the ability to rule over certain things. They are also to exercise judgment for the purpose of correction, teaching the nations of the earth the ways of God. These overcomers have been beheaded (had their carnal minds removed and replaced by the mind of Christ), not having worshipped the beast, his image, or his mark. This refers to the fact that these blessed and holy participants have shed their beast nature (put on the divine nature), been made into the image of God, and have shunned the mark of religion (the traditions and doctrines of men), pressing toward the mark for the prize of the high calling of God in Christ Jesus.

Everything up to this point which has been discussed pertaining to *the prize of the high calling of God in Christ Jesus* has been in reference to the idea that there is a prize, and that we are pressing into this calling to obtain it. The passage we have just quoted on the first resurrection, though, gives us information not only pertaining to the idea that there is a first resurrection to be obtained, but it also brings us beyond the obtaining of the prize, introducing us to the purpose which is behind this special reward.

Kings And Priests / Reigning With Him:

Revelation 20:6 states…"but they shall be **priests** of God and of Christ…" As well, Revelation 5:10 states…"(Jesus) has made us unto our God **kings** and **priests**: and we shall reign on the earth." In simple terms, to be a **king** unto God is to go to the people on behalf of God, and to be a **priest** unto God is to go to God on behalf of the people. This is the result and manifestation of receiving the prize and crown of the Lord. As you can see, this prize is not given to be selfishly kept, but rather, it is given to be shared with all of God's creation for the purpose of delivering people from the bondage of corruption into the glorious liberty of the children of God. Paul spoke of this very thing in Romans 8:19-21. It states…"For the earnest expectation of the creature waits for the manifestation of the sons of God. For the creature was made subject to vanity, not willingly, but by reason of Him Who has subjected the same in hope, Because the creature itself also shall be delivered from the bondage of corruption into the glorious liberty of the children of God."

Can you now see how this manifestation of God's sons (and daughters) at the first resurrection is for the purpose of bringing deliverance to others? This is what it is all about…DELIVERANCE! This is what it has always been about! God is not on an ego trip, nor are those who truly serve Him. The genuine children of the Lord understand why they are pressing into the high calling of God. They know God has called them to be saviors (deliverers), and they are EXCITED about this calling, knowing what it will mean in terms of deliverance for the creation of God. As a matter of fact, this is what Obadiah spoke of in verse 21 of his book. It states…"And **saviors** shall come up on mount Zion to judge the mount of Esau; and the kingdom shall be the Lord's." **ISN'T THAT WONDERFUL?**

Let's take a moment to hear from the anointed words of J. Preston Eby as he addresses this very subject.

According to J. Preston Eby:

"As one has written: "In the sovereign operation of the Spirit of God upon mankind, there is the apprehending of those whom He chooses to become a part of His specific workings for this day. In every age He has selected those whom He wills, drawing them out and beyond the normal course of this world's living, and placing within them a Divine Call, a sense of destiny which must be fulfilled. This inworking of His grace results in the formation of a 'new creation species' which becomes part of that 'firstfruits' for the demonstration of His love and salvation for all mankind. It is clearly written, 'And it was of His own will that He gave us birth as sons by His Word of Truth, so that we should be a kind of firstfruits of His creatures - A SAMPLE of what He created to be consecrated to Himself' (James 1:18, Amplified). Hence this divine selectivity is a vital part of the outworking of His own purpose, not for the excluding of all men from His salvation, but rather for the consummation of that plan, as they become instruments through whom His grace and mercy are revealed to others."

To these the word of promise is given: "You shall be a PECULIAR TREASURE unto Me above all people." Many of us know all too well that this word "peculiar" has often been used to cloak religious conduct both strange and irrational. People have been known to dress in outmoded or unusual styles of clothing, to act in wild and curious ways, and to do rather weird things and then grin a self-conscious grin and justify it all by saying, "Well, we are called to be God's peculiar people!" The English word "peculiar" in the language of A.D. 1611 (when the King James Bible was published) had no connotation of queerness, oddness, ridiculousness nor foolishness. It translates the Hebrew word GULLA meaning "to shut up wealth - to put the jewels, treasures, etc. belonging to a king in a safe, protected place because of their extraordinary value." It was God's way of emphasizing that His special people would be of great importance, value, and purpose to Him - a treasure above all other treasures.

Every loving mother and father has a good idea of what God meant. There are babies in houses up and down every street, as you can tell by the baby clothes hanging on the lines of a summer day. But in the house where you live, there is one little infant in particular, and he is a peculiar treasure unto you above all others. It does not mean necessarily that he is prettier, but it does mean that he is the treasure above all other treasures, full of hope and purpose in your lives, and you would not trade him for any other child in the whole world. He is a peculiar treasure! This gives us some idea, at least, of what we are – God's special jewels marked out for Him!

But it means infinitely MORE than that! The apostle Peter, reiterating the covenant of Ex. 19:5-6 states, and the Diaglott beautifully renders, "But you are a chosen Race, a Royal Priesthood, a holy Nation, a PEOPLE FOR A PURPOSE; that you may declare the Perfections of Him Who called you from darkness into His wonderful light." In the phrase, "a people FOR a purpose," it has been pointed out that the word "for" is the Greek word "eis" meaning INTO, and signifies that forward action of God taking a people and leading them onward, preparing them, purifying them, until they become merged into ONE with His purpose and reality. A people INTO A PURPOSE! So many wander through their whole lifetime here upon earth with no aim, no vision, no goal, no purpose for living, no understanding as to the why of this schooling experience under the dealing of God's hands, and no preparation for what lies beyond…

I cannot emphasize too strongly the important truth that ALL PRIESTHOOD has a double outreach - ministry to both God and man. It could not be otherwise, for a priest is one who "stands between" two factions in mediation, and the moment a priest ceases to touch both God and man, unifying the two, he simply ceases to be a priest. He may be a worshipper who speaks to God, or a king who rules the people for God, or a prophet who speaks on behalf of God, but no man can have a one-sided ministry and be a priest. The priest must minister unto God on behalf of men and unto men on behalf of God. The priest must touch God with one hand and mankind with the other hand, bringing the two together by his ministration. Anything less or different than this is not priesthood at all…

God has always wanted a priesthood. The priesthood is foundational to the outworking of His redemption and central to His plan of the ages. The covenant of God still stands today: "Now therefore, if you will obey My voice indeed, and keep My covenant, then you shall be A PECULIAR TREASURE UNTO ME ABOVE ALL PEOPLE: for all the earth is Mine: AND YOU SHALL BE UNTO ME A KINGDOM OF PRIESTS, AND AN HOLY NATION." Oh, beloved, come, let us now open our hearts wide to Him. Come, and as we gaze upon this glorious ministry and its life-flow to all the families of the earth, let us yield ourselves unto God that He may work His wondrous work in our lives, bringing us into such union with Jesus, the High Priest of our profession, that we become in nature and power His ROYAL PRIESTHOOD in the earth! The manifestation of the Sons of God for which all creation is in travail is nothing more nor less than the full manifestation of God's fully developed and empowered body of KING-PRIESTS AFTER THE ORDER OF MELCHISEDEK. Those apprehended unto this ministry are indeed, **A PEOPLE FOR A PURPOSE!**" -end quote- (The Royal Priesthood, J. Preston Eby)

How wonderful it is to know God is going to have a people for a purpose that shall rule and reign with Him a thousand years and beyond. The word "reign" (as used in Revelation 20:6) means *to exercise kingly power, control, or influence*. We are also told in Revelation 2:26-27 that the overcomers shall rule the nations. It states…"And he that overcomes, and keeps My works unto the end, **to him will I give power over the nations: And he shall rule them** with a rod of iron; as the vessels of a potter shall they be broken to shivers: even as I received of My Father." The word "rule" in this passage means *to feed, tend a flock, keep sheep, to rule, and govern*. How beautiful is the meaning of this word, for it portrays the loving heart of our Father in and through His king-priest company to be extended to all the nations of the earth. This word ("rule") implies the whole office of the shepherd, guiding, guarding, folding of the flock as well as leading it to nourishment. By now, it should be obvious that God's purpose of the ages in having a people to rule and reign is not to destroy the earth or its inhabitants, but to correct, reconcile, and restore all things unto Himself.

SUBMISSION TO SANCTIFICATION…THE MEANS BY WHICH GOD QUALIFIES US

According to Billy Thompson:

"One of the most controversial subjects in Christian religion is sanctification. It is when we have a "Pentecostal experience" where God gives us the earnest of His Spirit. At "Passover" God floods your spirit with His Spirit and it awakens the Christ in you. The Christ in you is perfect, but you are in need of understanding in your spirit. You are a babe in Christ and you are going to need some training to mature you. But you have two more components called soul and body that need to come into submission to the Christ in you." -end quote- (Billy Thompson)

Since man is spirit, soul, and body, we must approach this subject from this standpoint. In essence, our spirit is awakened by God at the time He gives us the faith to believe on the Lord Jesus Christ. This is referred to as "justification by faith" (Romans 5:1). This could be likened unto a person awaking from sleep to find out something has been accomplished for them that has now been made available and can be accessed due to the fact they have been awakened to what has been accomplished. Once we are awakened to believe on the Lord Jesus Christ it is imperative that we come to understand "what is the hope of God's calling, and what the riches of the glory of His inheritance in the saints, and what is the exceeding greatness of His power toward us who believe (Ephesians 1:18-19)." In other words, what is the purpose of being saved (justified by faith)? Most Christians teach that God has saved us to keep us from going to an eternal hell. This is definitely not what the Scriptures teach, and is therefore incorrect. The true message of the Bible tells us that we have been justified in order to then be sanctified and glorified. During our time of sanctification God causes our soul (mind, will, and emotions) to come in line with Him. Those who recognize and submit to this process are the ones who will be classified as overcomers, obtaining the prize of the first resurrection.

Can you imagine a coach of any sport allowing one of his players to be on the starting team if that player refuses to show up for practice, conditioning, or training? It would not happen! If a player refuses to be trained with his team, then he will simply be put on the bench and not be able to play on game day. It is just that simple…PERIOD! Well…This is how God deals with those who are to be put in positions of leadership. He trains us. It is in and through our time of sanctification that we are trained and qualified for the prize of the high calling of God in Christ Jesus.

Many would ask the question…What do you mean by sanctified? In order to grasp this concept it is necessary and helpful to have some understanding of the feasts of the Lord. The three major feasts of the Lord in the Old Testament are: Passover, Pentecost, and Tabernacles.

According to Dr. Stephen Jones:

"When God led Israel out of Egypt into the wilderness and into the Promised Land, He instituted various holidays, or "feast days" to commemorate important events. The three main feast days are Passover, Pentecost, and Tabernacles. Passover commemorates Israel's departure from Egypt; Pentecost commemorates the day God descended upon Mt. Sinai to give Israel the Law; Tabernacles commemorates the time Israel was supposed to cross the Jordan and enter the Promised Land.

It is very important that Christians study these feast days in detail, because they reveal the plan of God for the entire earth on a grand scale. They also reveal the plan of salvation on the individual level. The story written by Moses is not only history, but also is a great allegorical novel by which we can know the mind of God." -end quote- (The Barley Overcomers, Dr. Stephen Jones)

With these things in mind, let us focus on the Feast of Pentecost and its personal application for us as believers, for this feast is what we are to partake of (spiritually speaking) in order to be sanctified and qualified for the prize of the Lord. To explain how the Feast of Pentecost applies to us today, we must understand that this feast has its roots in the giving of the law of God. This represents the truth that God (by His Spirit) is writing His law (the law of the Spirit of life in Christ Jesus - God's character and nature) in our inward parts, and in our hearts (Jeremiah 31:33). After we have this revealed to us, we then become accountable to God to willingly submit to His process of training for the purpose of purification. During this time we are subjected to wilderness experiences in God, in which we are led by the Spirit into the wilderness (Luke 4:1) to be tempted of the Devil (the carnal mind). The purpose for this is not to destroy us, but to teach us how to access God's divine nature and overcome all that is contrary to His nature and character. God will use many different things to burn up our wood, hay, and stubble (carnality), such as fiery trials, afflictions, principalities and powers (rulers and authorities), subjecting us to vanity, and persecution from others. The important thing in all of this is to recognize that God is the One in control, and that if we continue to submit to this process, then we will be exalted (in due time), becoming profitable for the Master's use.

Remember…The whole point of being sanctified by the hand of the Lord is to have our iniquity (lawlessness) taken away from us. A good example given by Jesus concerning Christians who were justified but not sanctified is to be found in Matthew 7:21-23. It states…"Not every one that says unto Me, Lord, Lord, shall enter into the kingdom of heaven; but he that does the will of My Father which is in heaven. Many will say to Me in that day, Lord, Lord, have we not prophesied in Your name? and in Your name have cast out devils? and in Your name done many wonderful works? And then will I profess unto them, I never knew you: depart from Me, you that work iniquity (lawlessness)."

Contrary to popular belief, this passage does not mean that God is going to excommunicate these people and torture them forever. **It simply means they will be disqualified for the prize.** They are disqualified on the basis of not having submitted to God's process of sanctification. While they may have been very "churchy", they did not put on the character and nature of their Heavenly Father. When Jesus mentioned that He never knew these people, He was clearly referring to not knowing them in the area of sanctification (The Feast of Pentecost). They are classified as "workers of iniquity" because they have not submitted themselves to the consuming fire of God (God's fiery law) for the purpose of the destruction of the flesh (their ways, carnality, and corrupt nature).

BILL BRITTON'S VISION OF THE HARNESS OF THE LORD

If there was ever an example of what we have taught in this article on being qualified for the prize, it would be the vision that Bill Britton had concerning <u>The Harness Of The Lord</u>. The vision consisted of two young colts who had witnessed horses pulling the King's carriage. The horses that were pulling the carriage were arrayed with bells on their feet and pom-poms on their harnesses, and they were standing still and quiet, waiting for the voice of the Master. They were disciplined, and would not move until the Master told them to move. The two young colts who witnessed this asked the horses to come and play with them in the open field, but the horses did not respond, and did not go with them. This left the two colts puzzled. They could not understand why the horses would not want to play, and why they would want to have that awful harness on them.

Later in the vision the scene changed and lariat nooses fell around the necks of the two colts. They were led off to the Master's corral for **training** and **discipline**. They were sad because it seemed they had lost their freedom, being put into a place of confinement for the purpose of training. They ran from fence to fence trying to get out, but they were unable to escape. The colts had little knowledge of the **responsibility** that was to be theirs if they would **submit** to this time of **discipline**. As time went on, one of the colts rebelled against the training and found a way out, jumping the fence and returning to the meadows of grass. The Master let him go and did not go after him, but rather, devoted His attention to the remaining colt. This colt, though he had the same opportunity to escape, decided to submit his own will and learn the ways of the Master. After the period of training was over the Master dropped a harness on the shoulders of the colt, putting him into an even greater confinement than before. Here are the words of Bill Britton as he explains a portion of his vision pertaining to the harness of the Lord…

"The scene changed and I saw the other colt standing on the side of a hill nibbling at some grass. Then across the fields, down the road came the King's carriage drawn by six horses. With amazement he saw that in the lead, on the right side, was his brother colt now made strong and mature on the good corn in the Master's stable. He saw the lovely pom-poms shaking in the wind, noticed the glittering gold bordered harness about his brother, heard the beautiful tinkling of the bells on his feet -- and envy came into his heart. Thus he complained to himself: "Why has my brother been so honored, and I am neglected? They have not put bells on MY feet nor pom-poms on MY head. The Master has not given

ME the wonderful responsibility of pulling His carriage, has not put about ME the gold harness. Why have they chosen my brother instead of me?" And by the Spirit the answer came back to me as I watched: **"Because one submitted to the will and discipline of the Master and one rebelled, thus has one been chosen and the other set aside."** -end quote- (The Harness Of The Lord, Bill Britton)

If you happen to be reading this right now, then it is quite possible that King Jesus is calling you into this process of training and sanctification so that you will be fit to pull the King's carriage (metaphorically speaking). The first step is simply to recognize that this period of training is ordained by God and is designed to qualify you to stand (at the first resurrection) in the office of a king and a priest unto God on behalf of all the people of the earth. Oh what a calling it is. It is a heavenly, upward, and high calling. Ask God to give you the ability to simply understand the hope of this calling, and to submit and partake of this great Feast of Pentecost, which is to lead you to the Feast of Tabernacles. Remember…Without this (submission to sanctification) there can be no sharing of God's glory, no sonship (the placing of a fully mature son of God).

That I may know Him, and the power of His resurrection, and the fellowship of His sufferings, being made conformable unto His death;

If by any means I might attain unto the resurrection of the dead.

Not as though I had already attained, either were already perfect: but I follow after, if that I may apprehend that for which also I am apprehended of Christ Jesus.

Brethren, I count not myself to have apprehended: but this one thing I do, forgetting those things which are behind, and reaching forth unto those things which are before,

I press toward the mark for the prize of the high calling of God in Christ Jesus.

(Philippians 3:10-14)

PART 15 - THE GREATNESS OF GOD

To attempt to tackle the subject of the greatness of God, one must either be crazy or inspired. There is really no way to do justice to His greatness with mere words, but when God reveals to you a glimpse of Who He is, then it becomes as fire shut up in your bones and you have to tell the world about it. Too much of our talk in Christianity is about man, what he must do, and how that our "poor little God" is trying His best to fix what Adam (supposedly) messed up. Well...HOGWASH! Dr. Harold Lovelace, who has been preaching these things for over fifty years, has inspired, does inspire, and continues to inspire me to talk about **THE GREATNESS OF GOD!** Many Christians talk of Jesus as their "personal" Savior. That, my friend, is a beautiful thought, but it is far too limited of a way to think in terms of our Savior. Not only is He your Savior, _**BUT HE IS THE SAVIOR OF THE WORLD!!!**_ It is time for the body of Christ to awake from its slumber concerning the knowledge of Who their God is. Our problem is simply this: WE DO NOT UNDERSTAND HOW GREAT OUR GOD IS! The leaders (for the most part) in Christianity have taken away "the key of knowledge" from the people and replaced it with a *system of manipulation, fear, and control*. My prayer for those of you who read this is that you will hear the call to come out of Babylon (confusion), realizing that God is greater than you have ever imagined.

GOD IS GREAT

Psalm 145:3 states..."Great is the Lord, and greatly to be praised; and **His greatness is unsearchable**." As I sit here and try to write on such a grand subject, I can hardly comment on just how great I believe our God is. However great we think He is...He is greater than that. However powerful we think He is...He is more powerful than that. I have wondered from time to time if it would be proper to say that God possesses an insane amount of power, and yet this description of His power would still be inadequate. I have searched for ways to describe God's love, knowing all the while that my pitiful and pathetic words can never even come close to capturing the essence of the magnificent love of Jesus. One thing I do know, though, is that we must declare the greatness of God to the best of our ability, even if we do not possess the vocabulary to properly represent Him. Matthew Henry felt the same way. Here are some comments from his Bible commentary.

According to Matthew Henry:

"We must declare, *Great is the Lord,* His presence infinite, His power irresistible, His brightness insupportable, His majesty awful, His dominion boundless, and His sovereignty incontestable; and therefore there is no dispute, but *great is the Lord, and,* if great, then *greatly to be praised,* with all that is within us, to the utmost of our power, and with all the circumstances of solemnity imaginable. His greatness indeed cannot be comprehended, for it is unsearchable; who can conceive or express how great God is? But then it is so much the more to be praised. When we cannot, by searching, find the bottom, we must sit down at the brink, and adore the depth, Rom. 11:33. God is great, for, (1.) His majesty is glorious in the upper world, above the heavens, where He has set His glory; and when we are declaring His greatness we must not fail to *speak of the glorious honour of His majesty,* the splendour of the glory of His majesty (v. 5), how brightly He shines in the upper world, so as to dazzle the eyes of the angels themselves, and oblige them to cover their faces, as unable to bear the lustre of it. (2.) His works are wondrous in this lower world. The preservation, maintenance, and government of all the creatures, proclaim the Creator very great. When therefore we declare His greatness we must observe the unquestionable proofs of it, and must *declare His mighty acts* (v. 4), *speak of His wondrous works* (v. 5), *the might of His terrible acts,* v. 6. We must see God acting and working in all the affairs of this lower world. Various instruments are used, but in all events God is the supreme director; it is He that performs all things. Much of His power is seen in the operations of His providence (they are *mighty acts,* such as cannot be paralleled by the strength of any creature), and much of His justice—they are *terrible acts,* awful to saints, dreadful to sinners. These we should take all occasions to speak of, observing the finger of God, His hand, His arm, in all, that we may marvel." -end quote- (Matthew Henry's Commentary On The Whole Bible, Matthew Henry)

It is also interesting to note how the apostles spoke of the "wonderful works of God" in the book of Acts when they spoke in tongues on the day of Pentecost. Acts 2:4 states…"And they were all filled with the Holy Ghost, and began to speak with other tongues, as the Spirit gave them utterance. Now…Let us jump over to verse eleven, which states…"we do hear them speak in our tongues **the wonderful works of God.**" Verse five of that chapter tells us "there were dwelling at Jerusalem Jews, devout men, out of every nation under heaven." When the apostles spoke in tongues (tongues which could be recognized by those present) they spoke of the greatness of God. Some other translations refer to this as: the wonders of God, the mighty deeds of God, the mighty works of God, the great things of God, and the magnificent things of God. Oh what a great God we serve! The Spirit of God speaking through these men in other tongues had plenty of opportunity to speak of doom and gloom, negative things, and how mad God was to "supposed" to have been at the human race for their condition of sin. BUT NO...God spoke of His greatness, including His magnificent purpose and plan, which was later spoken of by Peter again when he said..."God will pour out of His Spirit upon ALL FLESH!" (Acts 2:17)

Since we have already determined the greatness of God to be a subject far beyond us having the ability to fully explain it, we will attempt to mention and develop a few key elements of His greatness, realizing that this will but introduce us to how big, awesome, wonderful, powerful, and loving our Heavenly Father is. Having said that, let us focus our attention on these two ideas:

1. GOD IS SOVEREIGN (ALL-POWERFUL, ALMIGHTY, INDISPUTABLE)

2. GOD IS LOVE (INESCAPABLE, NEVER-FAILING, AND ALL-LOVING)

THE GREATNESS OF GOD'S SOVEREIGNTY

Romans chapters 9, 10, and 11, which speak of the greatness of God's sovereignty, end with a climactic statement by the apostle Paul that starts in Romans 11:33. Paul states..."O the depth of the riches both of the wisdom and knowledge of God! how unsearchable are His judgments, and His ways past finding out! For who has known the mind of the Lord? or who has been His counselor? Or who has first given to Him, and it shall be recompensed unto him again? For of Him, and through Him, and to Him, are all things: to Whom be glory for ever. Amen.

Since this statement by Paul concludes his passage on the sovereignty of God, then we can be sure that whatever this statement means declares the purpose and intent of God in exercising His sovereignty over man. In other words, what is the result of God being sovereign in the affairs of men? The result is clearly stated in Romans 11:32, which states..."For God has concluded them all (Jews and Gentiles) in unbelief, THAT HE MIGHT HAVE MERCY UPON ALL." It also tells us in Romans 11:36 that "to Him (returning to God), are ALL THINGS..." This is how God chooses to use His sovereignty. He uses it to have mercy on all men, causing all to return to Him restored, corrected, and made in His image.

How is it that we should define the sovereignty of God? Is it correct to say God is all-powerful? Is it right to say God is almighty? Are we to understand that God has unlimited and indisputable power? Yes, yes, and yes. But let's define His sovereignty in even greater detail. Romans 9:16-24 is an amazing explanation by the apostle Paul concerning the sovereignty of God. It states…"**So then it is not of him that wills, nor of him that runs, but of God that shows mercy.** For the scripture says unto Pharaoh, Even for this same purpose have I raised you up, that I might show My power in you, and that My name might be declared throughout all the earth. Therefore has He mercy on whom He will have mercy, and whom He will He hardens. You will say then unto me, Why does He yet find fault? For who has resisted His will? Nay but, O man, who are you that replies against God? Shall the thing formed say to Him that formed it, Why have You made me thus? Has not the potter power over the clay, of the same lump to make one vessel unto honor, and another unto dishonor? What if God, willing to show His wrath, and to make His power known, endured with much longsuffering the vessels of wrath fitted to destruction: And that He might make known the riches of His glory on the vessels of mercy, which He had afore prepared unto glory, Even us, whom He has called, not of the Jews only, but also of the Gentiles?"

Many come away from a passage like this in awe of the sovereignty, power, and greatness of God…and so we should. But what about the mercy factor of God's sovereignty? It is little mentioned by many who bask in the idea of a sovereign God. Did it not say that GOD SHOWS MERCY? When this statement is put together with what Paul said in Romans 11:32 it becomes quite obvious that what makes God so great is not just that He is sovereign, BUT THAT HE USES HIS SOVEREIGNTY TO SHOW MERCY TO ALL! **Remember…God has made all men prisoners of disobedience, that He might have mercy upon all**. If He was sovereign alone, but did not show mercy to all, then He would have to be viewed as a cruel Creator. But thank God that He is not a cold-hearted monster as portrayed by many in the realm of Christianity. He is sovereign and merciful. HE IS GREAT! To this we say…Great is the Lord, and greatly to be praised; and **His greatness is unsearchable**.

THE GREATNESS OF GOD'S LOVE

The greatness of God's love goes far beyond mere human words. It is so grand that the human tongue and pen can hardly tell of its magnificence. The great song "The Love Of God" (written by Frederick Lehman) attests to this very thing…

The love of God is greater far
Than tongue or pen can ever tell;
It goes beyond the highest star,
And reaches to the lowest hell;
The guilty pair, bowed down with care,
God gave His Son to win;
His erring child He reconciled,
And pardoned from his sin.

Refrain

O love of God, how rich and pure!
How measureless and strong!
It shall forevermore endure
The saints' and angels' song.

When years of time shall pass away,
And earthly thrones and kingdoms fall,
When men, who here refuse to pray,
On rocks and hills and mountains call,
God's love so sure, shall still endure,
All measureless and strong;
Redeeming grace to Adam's race—
The saints' and angels' song.

Refrain

Could we with ink the ocean fill,
And were the skies of parchment made,
Were every stalk on earth a quill,
And every man a scribe by trade,
To write the love of God above,
Would drain the ocean dry.
Nor could the scroll contain the whole,
Though stretched from sky to sky.

Of all the men that walked with Jesus, John was the one called to write about the greatness of God's love more so than any other man. In his first epistle he describes **love** and **God** as being synonymous. 1ˢᵗ John 4:7-11 states…"**Beloved, let us love one another: for love is of God; and every one that loves is born of God, and knows God. He that loves not knows not God; for God is love. <u>In this was manifested the love of God toward us, because that God sent His only begotten Son into the world, that we might live through Him.</u> Herein is love, not that we loved God, but that He loved us, and sent His Son to be the propitiation for our sins. Beloved, if God so loved us, we ought also to love one another.**"

As you can see, not only is God love, but the greatness of His love was **manifested** to us in and through the sending of His Son. And we know that God sent His Son to be crucified and raised again to make atonement for the sin of the world. So…The greatness of God's love was manifested in the person of the Lord Jesus Christ, in that He gave His life to reconcile the human race back to the Father. Naturally, this leads us to talk about the greatness of the blood of the cross of Christ, which will ultimately draw (drag) all men unto Jesus.

THE GREATNESS OF THE CROSS OF CHRIST

It is amazing how we as Christians have found ways for centuries to explain away direct statements in Scripture which declare the greatness of God. We always end up placing too much emphasis on man's will, leaving us unable to understand the greatness of God's never-failing love and His absolute sovereignty. Jesus made a statement which is recorded in the book of John concerning this very thing. When this statement is accepted for what it truly is - a declaration of God's unlimited love and power through the cross of Christ - it truly makes a person free. Remember…You shall know the truth, and the truth shall make you free (John 8:32)! Are you ready for the truth? Well…Here it is…1ˢᵗ John 12:32-33 states…"**And I, if I be lifted up from the earth, will draw all men unto Me. This He said, signifying what death He should die.**" As well, here is the same verse from the Amplified Bible. It states…"**And I, if and when I am lifted up from the earth [on the cross], will draw and attract all men [Gentiles as well as Jews] to Myself. He said this to signify in what manner He would die.**"

Most who read these verses of Scripture fail to grasp this obvious, plain, and direct statement from the Lord Jesus. They immediately begin to put their emphasis on man's ability to lift up the Lord Jesus in worship and preaching, saying…"As we lift Him up in worship and preaching, men will be drawn to Him." While this may be true, this is clearly not what Jesus was talking about. When He said…"If I be lifted up from the earth", He was no doubt talking about His death on the cross. It tells us point blank…"This He said, signifying what death He should die." As a matter of fact, this Scripture is really not up for interpretation, as much as it is to be believed or not believed. It is as simple as that! If Jesus died on the cross (which He did, and was also raised from the dead three days later), THEN HE WILL DRAW ALL MEN UNTO HIMSELF! You can believe this or not, but it is not going to change the fact that it is going to happen, **and I am so glad there is nothing we can do about that**! Jesus will draw all men unto Himself in the fullness of time.

The word "draw" used in John 12:32 means: **to drag**. Oh what a powerful and loving Savior we serve! Some will rejoice after hearing these things, and others will gnash their teeth, insisting that *man's will* to be lost is more powerful than *God's ability* to save them. Others will trumpet their message of a "so-called free will", which is supposed to make man more powerful than God, giving Him the ability to resist the greatness of God's power and love. To that I say…"I DON'T THINK SO!" No one will be able to resist the greatness of God's power and love when they are revealed in all of their fullness. Remember…"That at the name of Jesus every knee should bow, of things in heaven, and things in earth, and things under the earth; And that every tongue should confess that Jesus Christ is Lord, to the glory of God the Father." (Philippians 2:10-11)

According to John Gavazzoni: (in response to those who see man's will as stronger than God)

"Now some, completely indoctrinated by the dumbed-down notion of free will, upon being confronted with what I've just shared, without any depth of thought at all, would accuse me of making man out to be a mere robot. But, I ask, if God has a free will, and brings man into participation with that will, how can freedom be defined as robotic? Freedom by definition, involves not being controlled by another.

The relationship of God's will to us, is not one of making us do something against our will, but by bringing our will into union with His. This is not coercion, this is causation, and it is causation by the force of love which ultimately worked by God leaving us to ourselves to do what we would do left to ourselves; which was to crucify His Son, and then to love such enemies back to Himself by the power of forgiving love to the praise of the glory of His grace." -end quote- (Free Will, John Gavazzoni)

WITH GOD, 99 IS NOT ENOUGH

The very reason Jesus was sent to this earth by the Father was to seek and save that which was lost (Luke 19:10). This would naturally lead us to ask the question…"What was *it* that was lost?" What was lost was…THE HUMAN RACE (ADAM'S RACE). The next question we must ask (which we have already asked and answered) is…"Did Jesus seek and save that which was lost?" The parable of the lost sheep is one of the many illustrations in the Bible which also brings across this all-important point. It is to be found in Luke 15:1-7. It states…"Then drew near unto Him all the publicans and sinners for to hear Him. And the Pharisees and scribes murmured, saying, This man receives sinners, and eats with them. And He spoke this parable unto them, saying, What man of you, having an hundred sheep, if he lose one of them, does not leave the ninety and nine in the wilderness, and go after that which is lost, until he find it? And when he has found it, he lays it on his shoulders, rejoicing. And when he comes home, he calls together his friends and neighbors, saying unto them, Rejoice with me; for I have found my sheep which was lost. I say unto you, that likewise joy shall be in heaven over one sinner that repents, more than over ninety and nine just persons, which need no repentance."

This parable (along with the parable of the lost coin and lost son) reveals to us the heart of our Heavenly Father. It shows us God's relentless tenacity, in that He will pursue every lost sheep until all are brought back to His loving arms. He refuses to give up on anyone, including those who would be characterized as His enemies. Psalm 66:3-4 tells us once again of the GREATNESS OF GOD'S POWER TO CAUSE HIS ENEMIES TO SUBMIT TO HIM! It states…"Say unto God, How terrible (awe-inspiring) are You in Your works! **through the greatness of Your power shall Your enemies submit themselves unto You**. All the earth shall worship You, and shall sing unto You; they shall sing to Your name. Selah." Sounds like God is going to get every last person to me! *The truth of the matter is: IT IS RESIDENT IN THE VERY NATURE AND CHARACTER OF GOD THAT IT IS IMPOSSIBLE FOR HIM TO LOSE ANYONE OR ANYTHING THAT CAME OUT FROM HIM! HE JUST CANNOT AND WILL NOT BE DEFEATED BY MAN'S POOR, PATHETIC, AND PUNY WILL. THE GREATNESS OF HIS POWER AND LOVE (WHEN REVEALED TO ALL MEN IN THE FULLNESS OF TIME) WILL BE IRRESISTIBLE AND INESCAPABLE!*

The following people are quoted in this book. The teachings in which they are quoted are listed after their name. If the quote came from a specific book, article, or work it is listed after the quote.

Abbott, Louis: Part 6

Amirault, Gary: Part 13

Britton, Bill: Part 9, Part 14

Crouch, Andre: Part 10

Eby, J. Preston: Part 3, Part 5, Part 6, Part 12, Part 14

Eldredge, Niles: Part 1

Gavazzoni, John: Part 7, Part 10, Part 15

Henry, Matthew: Part 15

Hitching, Francis: Part 1

Jackson, Wayne: Part 9

Jastrow, Robert: Part 1

Jones, Dr. Stephen: Part 8, Part 9, Part 10, Part 13, Part 14

LaPointe, Doug: Part 1

Lehman, Frederick: Part 15

Lovelace, Dr. Harold: Part 3, Part 12

Ruse, Michael: Part 1

Snipes, Eddie: Part 1

Thompson, Billy: Part 5, Part 14

ORDER FORM

THE NOBLE BEREAN SERIES VOLUME 2

Send this form, a photocopy of this form or a letter containing the information requested below to:

Straightway Publishing Company
P.O. Box 45212 #261
Baton Rouge, LA. 70895

Enclose a check or money order for $12.95, payable to Straightway Publishing Company. Straightway Publishing Company will pay shipping and handling and any sales taxes.

Fill in name and address where the book is to be shipped:

Name:_____

Address:_____

City:_____ State:_____ Zip:_____

In case of questions concerning your order, please give your phone number and Email address:

Telephone:_____

Email address:_____

If you have any questions, Straightway Publishing Company can be reached by calling (225) 766-0896.

*If this book is unsatisfactory for any reason
you may return it for a full refund.*

http://www.hearingthetruthofgod.com/

Printed in the United States
204849BV00004B/70-117/P